D0063053

CONNECTED
TO CHRIST

Overcoming Isolation
through Community

BRIAN K. DAVIES

CONCORDIA PUBLISHING HOUSE · SAINT LOUIS

For my mom, Linda—ever in my corner, relentlessly positive, and a great audience for my jokes. I love how much alike we are; I pray to have the influence on so many that you've had.

For my dad, Roy—*"I will see you again and we will rejoice, and no one will take away our joy"* (John 16:22, paraphrased).

For my wife, Beth—everyone needs someone to help them envision what we ourselves don't have the courage to see. Thanks for being that, and so much more, for me. *"Many women have done excellently, but you surpass them all"* (Proverbs 31:29).

Published by Concordia Publishing House
3558 S. Jefferson Ave., St. Louis, MO 63118-3968
1-800-325-3040 · cph.org

Manufactured in the United States of America

Library of Congress Cataloging-in-Publication Data

Names: Davies, Brian K., 1980, author.

Title: Connected to Christ : overcoming isolation through community / Brian Davies.

Description: Saint Louis : Concordia Publishing House, [2021] | Includes bibliographical references.

Identifiers: LCCN 2020039963 (print) | LCCN 2020039964 (ebook) | ISBN 9780758666932 (paperback) | ISBN 9780758666949 (ebook)

Subjects: LCSH: Communities--Religious aspects--Christianity. | Fellowship--Religious aspects--Christianity.

Classification: LCC BV4517.5 .D39 2021 (print) | LCC BV4517.5 (ebook) | DDC 250--dc23

LC record available at https://lccn.loc.gov/2020039963

1 2 3 4 5 6 7 8 9 10   30 29 28 27 26 25 24 23 22 21

Pastor Davies's book could not come at a more crucial time as the pandemic reveals how much we need and depend on being with one another in community. I appreciate how Pastor Davies frames the idea of community within our culture today as well as in God's story. The biblical examples he offers help guide readers through the importance of community and why God desires it for us. Stories from his ministry and examples from our world today round out a great resource for church leaders to help their communities deepen their relationships. The reflection questions at the end of each chapter are insightful and will help readers process the book as well as stir up great conversations.

Chip May, executive director, Camp Arcadia

Connected to Christ: Overcoming Isolation through Community is the perfect book at the perfect time. We live in a world of technology that is designed to connect us, yet somehow we have ended up more isolated than ever before. And now, we have a global pandemic that has moved us even further apart, away from one another and away from places of worship.

Brian Davies uses Scripture and real-life anecdotes to remind us of something so important—God calls us to live in community with one another, and He calls us to live our lives with compassion and mercy. The tools provided in this book are essential for all of us, especially in this moment. We need the Lord, and we need each other.

Connected to Christ: Overcoming Isolation through Community is a powerful and engaging call to action. We must reconnect with our communities. We must reconnect with our churches. This book will help us get there.

Marcus Leshock, news reporter and anchor, WGN-TV Chicago

It seems strange to assert that one of the most countercultural claims that we as Christians could make in twenty-first-century America is that we are created for community, but here we are: our society is scattered, tattered, and—despite the promises of technology--disconnected. Brian Davies incisively diagnoses our ills and demonstrates a more excellent way: connected to Christ and His Body, the Church. Read this book to recover a vision of what it looks like to live a life of faith in Christian community and to lead a body of believers that is bound both to the Lord and one another.

Rev. Dr. Ryan P. Tinetti, pastor, Trinity Lutheran Church, Arcadia, Michigan

Years ago, I ministered to a man enduring a terrible tragedy in his life. He was angry at God and struggling to keep his faith. In the midst of his immense pain, the church had rallied around him with love, support, encouragement, and prayers. Expressing his gratitude to me one day, he said, *"I'm not sure if I believe in Christ anymore, but I believe in the Body of Christ more than ever!"* Eventually, the love of the church helped him believe again in the love of Jesus. This book is going to help create more churches like that!

Rev. Scott Christenson, senior pastor, St. Paul's Lutheran Church and School,
Orange, California

Rev. Davies has written an inspirational book that points the Church back to its Acts foundation. *Connected to Christ* gives the Church vision and practical skills for overcoming isolation by establishing a vibrant community. Brian gives us some heartwarming stories of the power of the people of God coming alongside isolated people and loving them into a Christ-centered community. The book follows a simple plan. Brian dives into how community is found, realized, and practiced. He lays out how Jesus invites us to identity and belonging in Him, and how God has indeed made a space at the table for each of us. The book points out how the Lord's vision is that all who find identity and belonging in Him also find community with one another. Rev. Davies finally leads us to the practical ways to discover the richness of life together. This is a must-read book for anyone seeking an authentic community. If you follow the lessons in this book, it could create life-transformation in your church.

Rev. B. Keith Haney, assistant to the president for Missions,
Human Care, and Stewardship, Iowa West District LCMS

Brian does a tremendous job of helping us see the biblical call for community and why God has designed us for community. This book is so much more than just information, it is also inspiration that leads to genuine transformation. The theological depth, with the real-life application, makes this book one that is for everyone!

Rev. Greg Griffith, lead pastor, King of Kings Church, Omaha, Nebraska

CONTENTS

COMMUNITY, TWO WAYS

I was in a car with people who were strangers to me, and no one was saying much.

I was in the backseat. Becca and Jay were in the front seat of their vehicle, which was parked outside their home. Together, we watched their house go up in flames. My heart grieved for them and with them. As chaplain of the local fire department, I was called to the scene to talk with them and simply to be present with them. And so we sat, together, in their car. Occasionally, I'd reach up, put my hands on their shoulders, and offer a word of encouragement and hope.

I wish you could know Becca and Jay—they are awesome. Becca is quiet, super sweet, and very warmhearted. To this day, she texts me just to see how I'm doing. Jay is outgoing and has a great sense of humor. If he is in the room, everyone knows it. Even though no one calls me "Father" except my children, he took to calling me "Padre."

About two weeks after the fire, our church staff hosted a lunch for Becca and Jay. They are not members of our church and had never even been inside the building, but our staff heard me speak of them and their predicament and wanted to do something. The lunch gave Becca and Jay a respite from the grind of dealing with the insurance company and finding a place to live. It was the first time they set foot in our church, their first time in *any* church in a while.

As we ate and as Becca and Jay shared their story, there were moments of vulnerability and emotion on their part and genuine care from our staff. There were also, maybe surprisingly, a lot of laughs. Quickly, strangers became friends.

As our time together was winding down, Jay made a statement. We all watched intently as he took an empty pizza box in his hands and said, "For much of my life, I've had a hard time believing in God. I'm a tangible person, so I like things I can see and touch, like this pizza box. It was hard for me to believe in something I couldn't see and experience. But you all have helped me believe in God. You are the tangible way that God is real for us right now."

Is that awesome, or what?

Someone else I wish you could meet is a gentleman named Pete Hanson. Pete, in his early 70s, is full of energy and smiles easily. Just shy of their fiftieth wedding anniversary, his beloved Karen passed away. Pete had been an outstanding caregiver, and while he rejoiced that her struggle was over and she was with her Lord, he was now alone. He was hurting, and his church family knew it.

The day after Karen's funeral, Pete was in church, just like on any other Sunday. Of course, this time he came by himself and sat by himself. You can imagine that after decades of worshiping with Karen by his side, this first Sunday alone must have been difficult.

Yet here's the good part.

During the message, knowing what Pete had just been through and observing him by himself, our worship leader, Michael, did something really cool—he sat with Pete.

I stepped to the pulpit and began my message with a prayer. When I opened my eyes, I scanned the sanctuary and saw that Pete was no longer alone. Even as the words of my message were coming out of my mouth, inside my heart was overflowing with joy. This moment was so right.

And it gets better.

During the closing, Michael had to leave Pete to help finish the service. Again, Pete sat alone—but only for a moment. Marcus took Michael's place next to Pete. For the close of worship, twenty-something Marcus had his arm around seventy-something Pete.

Is that awesome, or what?

Two different stories, bound by a common theme—the power of community. That means finding a place of identity and belonging, being heard and cared for and known.

The desire to belong to a community that gives us our identity and cares for us is a longing of every human heart.

God created us with this desire. In fact, this picture of community is God's vision for His people and His Church.

This book is a call to discover (or rediscover) the power of community, because community *matters.* In our hyper-individualized, smartphone culture, people are longing to find a place of identity, connection, and belonging, but they aren't sure where that place is. *Connected to Christ* shows that when Jesus draws people to Himself, they find not only identity, connection, and belonging in Him, but they also find it in His Church. When the local congregation is at its best, it helps everyone—Pete, Becca and Jay, and you—find community.

My prayer is that this book

- renews your understanding of your place in God's family;
- leads you to anchor yourself in how He has made a place of identity and belonging for you; and
- ultimately helps you discover the beauty of being in this community.

Thank you for reading.

CHAPTER 1

CREATED FOR COMMUNITY

In 2018, the British Red Cross announced that it had identified a huge challenge facing its people "associated with a reduction in lifespan similar to that caused by smoking 15 cigarettes a day."[1] To address the growing crisis, the government created a new cabinet position to focus on it.

What crisis led to the appointment of a new cabinet position?

Loneliness. That's right. Along with cabinet positions to manage the defense, budget, foreign relations, education, and other critical aspects of government, the United Kingdom has a Loneliness Minister. And the problem is, this isn't limited to the United Kingdom.

Major health insurance provider Cigna recently completed a survey of more than twenty thousand adults in the United States, and their findings were also alarming. Part of

---

1   sitn.hms.harvard.edu/flash/2018/loneliness-an-epidemic/

the data broke down feelings of isolation and loneliness across different generations and age groups. Before I share the results, think for a moment—which demographic group would you expect to be the loneliest? I would have expected that older generations would report these feelings the most. After all, they often live alone, and we might not think of them as being in the socially prime season of life. However, the Cigna study reported that the oldest generations experienced the greatest sense of connection and well-being. Each subsequent generation felt increasingly lonely and isolated. Gen Z (those born from the mid-to-late 1990s to the early 2010s) reported the most loneliness and isolation.[2]

Those who are the most digitally connected feel the most alone.

So think about this: those who are the most digitally connected feel the most alone.

Upon reflection, and with some observation, this ought not surprise us. If you've been to an airport gate, school, or sports practice pickup, or really any gathering of humanity lately, you've seen it—people staring at their phones. Perhaps you've even seen it when two people are out together on a date.

This is not just a phone problem. The days of visiting with the neighbors, attending summer block parties, and waving

2   www.cigna.com/about-us/newsroom/studies-and-reports/loneliness-epidemic-america

to people from the front porch are replaced by pulling the car into the garage after work, retreating inside the house, and locking the doors. Places of community that used to be found and celebrated at legion halls, bowling alleys, bocce courts, and main streets have given way to a hyper-individualism and a culture of segmentation and division.

It doesn't feel right.

Sociologists have long pointed to the importance of a "third place" in our lives, separate from the social environments of home ("first place") and workplace ("second place"). For years, coffee giant Starbucks made a strong push for its stores to be this third place for customers and marketed itself as a place of community formation. Yet even Starbucks noted this tectonic culture shift. A March 2019 corporate press release pointed to a trend toward drive-through and delivery services, declaring about its customers, "Their third place is everywhere they're holding our cup."[3]

Bottom line—as a culture, we are losing our places of community, and it's doing a number on us. Feelings of isolation, loneliness, anxiety, and depression are rapidly increasing. And in the ultimate twist of irony, instead of being driven toward one another, we're drifting further and further apart. Much has been written about the present state of division and segmentation in American culture. Of all the

---

3 www.businessinsider.com/starbucks-reimagine-third-place-2019-3

anecdotes and statistics, I found this one the most compelling and symptomatic: In 1960, only 5 percent of Americans said they would be displeased if their child married someone from the other political party. By 2010, that number was 40 percent.[4] I'm afraid to think what the percentage is today.

Something's not right.

Not long ago, my wife and I pulled up to the grocery store. She wanted to run in and get something. Because it was going to be a quick visit, I stayed in our silver minivan, parked near the front entrance, right behind another vehicle that looked quite similar to ours. After a few minutes, a woman came out with a small bag of groceries and walked toward our minivans, studying her receipt. She approached our vehicle and . . . wait for it . . . opened the door and sat down. She started talking about her purchase, looked over, and immediately realized she was in the wrong van! While I tried to speak a word of consolation, I don't think she heard me—I've never seen someone exit a vehicle quicker!

Separating from other people is not the answer.

I tell you this because when it comes to finding identity, belonging, and community, we are getting into the wrong minivan. We need it, and we're seeking it, but separating from other people is not the answer.

4 madeinamericathebook.wordpress.com/2012/09/24/the-polarizing-political-paradox-redux/

Cultural observers see a rapid rise in what they call "tribalism," the segmentation and division of culture into sides or camps—"tribes." Perhaps you've also noticed that it seems every option puts you in one camp or another, everything from chicken sandwiches to sneakers, from news networks to hummus. We're united with some, divided from others. And while tribalism may give the appearance of community, under it is a divisiveness that has us looking at the "other" with disagreement, judgment, and even anger because much of what binds us together is what another group is against.

This attitude causes many to lament and rightfully so. Again, we see and feel like something is not right because this is not the way God designed us to be. Unfortunately, as God gets pushed further and further into the periphery of culture, this is the result. In a way, we're finding community at the expense of, or in opposition to, others. Meanwhile, Satan is laughing and rejoicing. It's as if Jesus was thinking of us when He said, "Every kingdom divided against itself is laid waste, and no city or house divided against itself will stand" (Matthew 12:25).

At the 2004 Athens Summer Games, American air-rifle shooter Matt Emmons entered the final leg of what's called the "three-position event" with a commanding lead. In the event, participants shoot from their stomachs, knees, and feet at a target fifty meters away. Going into the last of the three positions, Emmons needed only an average shot to take the gold. He lined up and nailed the target. Boom!

Only one problem. It was the wrong target!

Emmons nailed it, but he hit the target in one lane over. This "cross-fire" gave Emmons a score of zero, and he dropped from first place to eighth.

Emmons's story is gripping and heartbreaking because we know Olympic athletes dedicate so much to their skill. And because of the four-year Games schedule, they sometimes get only one opportunity to compete. For Emmons to work so hard and, up to the final event, so successfully and then to hit the wrong target must have been a frustrating blow.

We're seeking the target of identity, belonging, and community, but by breaking into tribes, we miss the very heart of the gift the Lord has for us in community.

That His creation would experience unity was important to Jesus. So much so, that when Jesus prayed while He was on earth, He prayed for us to have unity, belonging, and community. In John 17, right before He is arrested and is facing crucifixion, read what Jesus prayed:

> Holy Father, keep them in Your name, which You have given Me, that they may be one, even as We are one. . . . "I do not ask for these only, but also for those who will believe in Me through their word, that they may all be one, just as You, Father, are in Me, and I in You, that they also may be in Us, so that the world may

believe that You have sent Me. The glory that You have given Me I have given to them, that they may be one even as We are one, I in them and You in Me, that they may become perfectly one, so that the world may know that You sent Me and loved them even as You loved Me. (John 17:11, 20–23)

This is the prayer of our Lord Jesus for us. It is heart-breaking, then, that loneliness, isolation, division, and divisiveness reign among us.

Yet I have great hope, and this is a book of hope because it reminds us where to turn.

John 6 details a difficult moment, a turning point, early in the ministry of Jesus. He had just shared a difficult teaching, and many of those who had followed Jesus followed Him no longer. Jesus asks the Twelve if they also want to leave. Check out Peter's response:

[Jesus said,] "Do you want to go away as well?" Simon Peter answered Him, "Lord, to whom shall we go? You have the words of eternal life, and we have believed, and have come to know, that You are the Holy One of God." (John 6:67–69)

I have great hope because I believe that what our culture is longing for—identity, belonging, and community—can indeed be found. I wrote this book because there is a beautiful intersection between our human need for connection and community and God's vision for His people and His Church.

God created us to be in community; with His Church, He established a place for us to find it.

This fact is woven throughout the Scriptures. The concepts of community, connection, identity, and belonging are written into God's story from Genesis to Revelation. Track with me, and be on the lookout for community and connection. (If you're not familiar with the Bible, that's all right. Come along anyway, because community and connection are there for you too.)

Community in the Bible — A Quick Survey

- **It begins in the creation story, Genesis 1 and 2.** God looks at the pinnacle of His creation—humanity— and declares that it functions best with connection and community.

Then the LORD God said, "It is not good that the man should be alone; I will make him a helper fit for him." (Genesis 2:18)

A lot of information is contained in this one verse. It reveals that from the very beginning, God wired us for community. We were not meant to do life alone; we were not meant to experience the brokenness that comes through loneliness and isolation. That is, in the Bible's words, "not good."

Instead, God created "helpers" for us, people to be in our corner, loving and supporting us. These people are God's gifts to us, part of what He created for us. And these helpers aren't just any people—they are those whom God created as "fit" for us as pieces of a puzzle that fit together.

Reflect for a moment and consider: *Who are the people in this helper role for me? Who is uniquely in my corner?* Give thanks to God for them—they are gifts from Him to you!

- **The twelve tribes of Israel.** From very early on in the Old Testament, God places His people into tribes or communities. They were not meant to be alone but were to connect with God and to connect with one another throughout these tribes.

  And God said to him, "I am God Almighty: be fruitful and multiply. A nation and a company of nations shall come from you, and kings shall come from your own body." (Genesis 35:11)

Throughout the Old Testament, we see how essential these tribes were. Their tribe was who they *were*, an unchangeable part of their personal identity. Tribes provided grounding and belonging.

We function best in community because isolation is incredibly harmful to the human soul. There is no doubt that God knows this about us.

- **Jesus calling disciples.** Think about it—Jesus could have done His ministry alone. Solo. His ministry of teaching, healing, resurrecting, and so much more didn't need any helpers. Yet Jesus called people to follow Him, and in doing so, He invited them to find community with one another and, get this, with Him!

While walking by the Sea of Galilee, He saw two brothers, Simon (who is called Peter) and Andrew his brother, casting a net into the sea, for they were fishermen. And He said to them, "Follow Me, and I will make you fishers of men." Immediately they left their nets and followed Him. And going on from there He saw two other brothers, James the son of Zebedee and John his brother, in the boat with Zebedee their father, mending their nets, and He called them. Immediately they left the boat and their father and followed Him. (Matthew 4:18–22)

Jesus selected people to come alongside Him—to walk where He walked, to sit at His feet, to break bread with Him. They were a community, a tribe, following Jesus together. Jesus knew that the best way to mentor the folks who would be the leaders of the Early Church was to invite them into community with Him. Genius.

- **Jesus sending disciples.** The "internship" the disciples experienced in community with Jesus included not only following Him and taking notes but also being sent by Him to bear His message to surrounding towns and villages. And by sending them out, Jesus gives critical direction about how they would go:

And He called the twelve and began to send them out two by two, and gave them authority over the unclean spirits. He charged them to take nothing for their journey except a staff—no bread, no bag, no money in their belts—but to wear sandals and not put on two tunics. And He said to them, "Whenever you enter a house, stay there until you depart from there. And if any place will not receive you and they will not listen to you, when you leave, shake off the dust that is on your feet as a testimony against them." So they went out and proclaimed that people should repent. And they cast out many demons and anointed with oil many who were sick and healed them. (Mark 6:7–13)

Wouldn't it have made more sense, perhaps been more efficient, to send the disciples out alone? Think about it—they could have (theoretically) visited twice as many locations. Yet again, God the Son reveals how well He knows His creation. He knew the disciples would need each other, would need that community. Being a disciple would bring tough moments, and self-doubt would surely creep in. Jesus gave special attention to the fact that they shouldn't and wouldn't need "things"—food, clothing, money—but they *would* need companionship. He knew they would need each other. He knew they would need community.

- **Jesus in Gethsemane.** From my read of the New Testament, this is the only time Jesus asks His disciples to do something for Him. The totality of Jesus' other directives are to bless and benefit others. But here, Jesus asks something of them for Him.

Then Jesus went with them to a place called Gethsemane, and He said to His disciples, "Sit here, while I go over there and pray." And taking with Him Peter and the two sons of Zebedee, He began to be sorrowful and troubled. Then He said to them, "My soul is very sorrowful, even to death; remain here, and watch with Me." (Matthew 26:36–38)

In this hour of need, Jesus asked for support from His disciples. He knew the days ahead—His arrest, suffering, and crucifixion—would be so difficult, and He wanted them to hang with Him. *"Watch with Me."*

Jesus Himself knew the power of community. And if He reached out for community, shouldn't we do the same?

- **Community in the Early Church.** I love the scene Luke records for us in Acts 1, describing in beautiful detail the majestic ascension of Jesus. This is the moment Jesus returns to heaven, again taking His place at the Father's right hand. Luke records the disciples taking it all in, attempting to make sense of it. I picture them openmouthed as they stare into the sky. Take a quick look at the passage, and note the imperative of the angel, the messenger of God sent to them:

And when He had said these things, as they were looking on, He was lifted up, and a cloud took Him out of their sight. And while they were gazing into heaven as He went, behold, two men stood by them in white robes, and said, "Men of Galilee, why do you stand looking into heaven? This Jesus, who was taken up from you into heaven, will come in the same way as you saw Him go into heaven." (Acts 1:9–11)

In other words—don't just stand there. Get busy; you've got work to do!

And that work, fueled by the Holy Spirit who would descend upon them at Pentecost, was the formation of the Early Christian Church. From the very beginning, community was the foundation of the life they would lead together.

And they devoted themselves to the apostles' teaching and the fellowship, to the breaking of bread and the prayers. And awe came upon every soul, and many wonders and signs were being done through the apostles. And all who believed were together and had all things in common. And they were selling their possessions and belongings and distributing the proceeds to all, as any had need. And day by day, attending the temple together and breaking bread in their homes, they received their food with glad and generous hearts, praising God and having favor with all the people. And the Lord added to their number day by day those who were being saved. (Acts 2:42–47)

What a beautiful picture of the Early Church, the Church on earth at its very beginning, living in community. This passage in Acts shows that the people had a strong feeling of identity and belonging as they shared life together. This is how God designed the Church to be.

The remainder of the New Testament, which includes many letters to early Christians, reiterates the call to find and remain in community with one another. We'll look at a few of these later on, but consider now the urgency to remain in community that is expressed in the Book of Hebrews:

> Let us hold fast the confession of our hope without wavering, for He who promised is faithful. And let us consider how to stir up one another to love and good works, not neglecting to meet together, as is the habit of some, but encouraging one another, and all the more as you see the Day drawing near. (Hebrews 10:23–25)

As the Christian Church grew and as time went on, some people drifted away from fellowship and community. This is why the author of this letter impresses upon his readers how important it is "to stir up one another to love and good works" and to continue to meet together. It was imperative that to remain in the one true faith, they would need to remain in community.

One more, and it's worth it.

• **Looking ahead to heaven.** The end of the Bible, the Book of Revelation, paints a vivid scene that ought to give us great hope. It's a portrait of the entire Christian Church, from all times, gathered in one place at the second coming of the Lord Jesus Christ. Check it out, and see how it oozes community:

After this I looked, and behold, a great multitude that no one could number, from every nation, from all tribes and peoples and languages, standing before the throne and before the Lamb, clothed in white robes, with palm branches in their hands, and crying out with a loud voice, "Salvation belongs to our God who sits on the throne, and to the Lamb!" (Revelation 7:9–10)

What a scene! This is community, perfectly realized! What a powerful undoing of all the division the evil one has sowed in humanity since the dawn of creation. I imagine that a modern twist on this moment might go something like this:

A great multitude that no one could number from every political party, economic status, educational level, social media outlet, and cable news channel!

Won't that be wonderful!

I share these with you so you might see how the thread of community, identity, and belonging runs throughout the Bible from the very beginning to its end. That is how God designed us to live.

Despite all the fractured groups and division we see around us, community is God's idea and it absolutely *can* be realized today. God created us to seek and find identity and belonging; in Him, we find it!

In the coming chapters, we'll dive into how community is found, realized, and practiced. We'll see how Jesus invites us to identity and belonging in Him and how God has indeed made a space at the table for each of us. Then, we'll see how the Lord's vision is that all who find identity and belonging in Him also find community with one another. This is the Church. Then, we'll conclude by looking at ways to discover the richness of life together.

Community is God's idea and it absolutely can be realized today.

Let's go! God has called us—God has called *you*—to this!

Questions to invite reflection and conversation

1. In what ways do you sense loneliness and anxiety on the rise culturally?

2. Where do you see an increase of divisions and a spirit of divisiveness in our world today?

3. What impact is tribalism having on our culture? How is it leading us to think negatively about others?

4. Why do you think unity was so important to Jesus? Why did He pray to God the Father for it?

5. This chapter listed concepts of community that are found throughout the Bible. Which example was new or most striking to you?

CHAPTER 2

DO I FIT IN? THE INVITATION OF JESUS TO FIND COMMUNITY IN HIM

It's one of my favorite Bible stories and also a narrative that comes with a "don't try this at home" warning.

I'm referring to the story of the paralyzed man and his friends who wouldn't take no for an answer. (See Matthew 9:1–8; Mark 2:1–12; Luke 5:17–26.) Hearing that Jesus had come to their town (imagine that!), out of love for their paralyzed friend, they carried him to see Jesus. But when they get to the house where Jesus is, it's absolutely packed, a sea of people shoulder to shoulder. That's when one of them gets an idea . . .

MacGyver-style, they get themselves, and their friend, up to the roof of the home. In an act of love and courage for their friend, they cut a hole in the roof and use ropes to lower him into the house, right in front of Jesus.

I love this story because the paralyzed man had likely felt rejected, like an outsider. In first-century culture, a medical condition often meant exclusion from the greater community. Many thought that the ailment was caused by something the person had done, a sin that had brought God's judgment. We know this from the Gospel of John, where people ask of Jesus, "Rabbi, who sinned, this man or his parents, that he was born blind?" (John 9:2). So it's highly likely that the paralyzed man in this particular story felt like an outsider, that he felt unworthy and unacceptable to God.

Yet here he is, actually being lowered through the roof of a house to be face-to-face with God the Son.

And Jesus knows exactly what to say: "Man, your sins are forgiven you" (Luke 5:20).

In this moment, with His words, Jesus makes it so this man, regardless how culture had labeled him, was now in community with Him. The man's sins were forgiven, and he was now right with God. The blessings bestowed upon him would continue:

> He said to the man who was paralyzed—"I say to you, rise, pick up your bed and go home." And immediately he rose up before them and picked up what he had been lying on and went home, glorifying God. (Luke 5:24–25)

Through Jesus' spoken word of forgiveness and healing, this paralyzed man was no longer the paralyzed man but was the restored and forgiven man. Jesus single-handedly brought this man into community with Him, changing his life forever. In Jesus, he would now know identity and belonging in an entirely new way.

And perhaps my favorite part. He'd have a memento, a keepsake, to always remind him of God's grace made manifest in his life—his old bed.

The bed, which was less like a twenty-first-century mattress and more like a mat, the bed he lay on every single day of his life, would no longer serve that purpose. Instead, it would serve as a reminder of what he once was. It was something he would no longer need but could still treasure, a trophy of sorts. The mat reminded him: "I was once made to feel outside, but God brought me in."

This is a story of a paralyzed man, some good friends, and an awesome healing. It's also a story of so much more because many of us feel like that man.

The world does a phenomenal job of beating us up. Each of us is fed a steady diet of the ways we don't measure up. From performance reviews at work to grades at school, we are evaluated. Our culture encourages us to strive for achievement as personal validation, and when we fall short, it stings. We are in constant comparison to others; it seems like someone else is smarter, skinnier, more popular, more athletic, a better parent, or just plain better at life.

The twenty-sixth president of the United States, Theodore Roosevelt, said it best: *"Comparison is the thief of joy."*

This is especially difficult for young people, who are regularly bombarded with messages of comparison through social media. A feature of social networking is that people present only their best selves, their best moments. Thanks to social media, we know when everyone else is getting together and having fun without us. And when everyone else is seemingly always smiling and thriving, it can be difficult to come to grips with the valleys of our life. Feelings of loneliness, isolation, and inadequacy arise.

Yes, indeed, the world does a phenomenal job of beating us up.

And here's the critical part—we bring this into our relationship with God. We internalize that sense of inadequacy and not measuring up, and we drag it into our life with God. We bring that sense of striving for achievement into our life with God, hoping that the good we do might outweigh the bad.

For some of us, this perception of inadequacy is a result of our past. Perhaps we didn't grow up going to church, and so the stories everyone else seems to know are unfamiliar to us. Or perhaps there are things we've done, parts of our personal history, that we're embarrassed about. Both make us feel like we don't fit in, that we don't belong, in community with God.

For others, this sense of inadequacy is rooted in the present. Maybe we don't go to church much these days. We think there are church people who are "in," and we are "out." Perhaps this is how the paralyzed man felt before he met Jesus. Or it might be that we have thoughts, attitudes, or temptations that make us feel like we are on the outs with God.

I've heard this reflected in the comment, *"If I ever went back to church, the walls would cave in."* For the record, I assure you, they will not.

These feelings are the result of what we call God's Law. Wired within us is this knowledge of what should be, of what is true and right, and an insight that we don't measure up to it. The Old Testament prophet Jeremiah speaks to this, and it's quoted again in the New Testament in Hebrews 10:16.

> "I will put My law within them, and I will write it on their hearts." (Jeremiah 31:33)

God's Law is indeed written on our hearts. It's the moral code of life; it's how we can say something is right or wrong. The issue becomes what we do with it.

Some choose to deny it. They proclaim the myth that there is no such thing as absolute truth and instead say truth is relative and subjective. Hence, we get the term "your truth."

Others choose to ignore it. Life presents many distractions. The busyness of home, work, family, school, activities, and more can keep our minds quite full. And when we do get a few moments of downtime, streaming services and smartphones can take us to a different place.

I believe this book is in your hands because you are curious. Because you know you were made for more. I'd like to do for you what the friends of the paralyzed man did for him—I'd like you to take you to meet Jesus.

Illinois State Trooper Gerald Ellis had just completed his shift and was heading home on the highway. Not many were on the road in these early morning hours, but of those that were, one included a family. And in the distance was something strange and very wrong—a vehicle driving erratically and going the wrong way (later reports confirmed that the driver of this vehicle had a blood-alcohol content that was more than twice the legal limit). We can't know what happened in the moments before Ellis's patrol car swerved into the oncoming vehicle. But we can believe that Trooper Ellis gave his life so others could live.

This is what Jesus Christ came to do for you. He was a teacher, a revolutionary, a healer for sure, and so much more. But His primary and essential work was laying down His life for you. In this act of immeasurable courage and self-sacrifice, Jesus took upon Himself the punishment for sin that was due to us. Take a look at how the Bible describes it:

> For our sake He [God] made Him [Jesus] to be sin who knew no sin, so that in Him we might become the righteousness of God. (2 Corinthians 5:21)

And the best part—this gift is given to us not *because* of who we are or what we've done but *despite* who we are and what we've done! When we meet Jesus, just like the paralyzed man, we come with our imperfections and inadequacies and sin, and in light of all of this, a new word is spoken over us and changes us:

> Therefore, if anyone is in Christ, he is a new creation. The old has passed away; behold, the new has come. All this is from God, who through Christ reconciled us to Himself. (2 Corinthians 5:17–18)

I pray that you see for the first time, or perhaps see anew, the radically inclusive nature of the Gospel. The work of Jesus Christ brings us into a relationship, into community, with God, and it's solely based on what Jesus has done. The Gospel (another word for "good news") is not "clean yourself up and then you will be acceptable to God," but rather that God saw all our sin and brokenness and came down to us in the person of Jesus Christ, descending (being lowered down like the paralyzed man) into the muck and mire of our lives and making it so we can have peace with God.

Through Jesus Christ, you are brought into community with God. And God has ordained a sure and certain way that you can know this is true—Baptism.

Baptism, as one of the primary means and delivery points of God's grace, is a thread that runs throughout the Scriptures. In his Letter to the Church in Galatia, Paul speaks of life before and life after the gift of Baptism:

> Now before faith came, we were held captive under the law, imprisoned until the coming faith would be revealed. So then, the law was our guardian until Christ came, in order that we might be justified by faith. But now that faith has come, we are no longer under a guardian, for in Christ Jesus you are all sons of God, through faith. For as many of you as were baptized into Christ have put on Christ. (Galatians 3:23–27)

I love the image in 3:27; it is uniform language. In Baptism, Christ is "put on" us, and we are with Him and in Him. Other translations of this text speak of being "clothed" with Christ. In his Letter to the Romans, Paul develops this even further. He speaks of Baptism as a death and resurrection moment for us:

> Do you not know that all of us who have been baptized into Christ Jesus were baptized into His death? We were buried therefore with Him by baptism into death, in order that, just as Christ was raised from the dead

by the glory of the Father, we too might walk in newness of life. (Romans 6:3–4)

In Baptism, we have the certainty that He, the Lord Jesus Christ, makes us new, gives us a new identity.

At its foundation, Christianity is not a "do" religion—it is a "done" religion. There is nothing you can do to make God love you any more, and there is nothing you can do to make God love you any less. Jesus has made a place at the table for you, and Baptism is one sure and certain delivery point for this precious gift.

Christianity is not a "do" religion—it is a "done" religion.

In an oft-repeated story, Martin Luther is alone in the Wartburg, battling an internal monologue regarding his personal unworthiness and inadequacies. He senses the evil one trying to pull him deeper into doubt and despair. In that moment, he takes hold of his inkwell and throws it across the room. In his mind, he's throwing the inkwell at Satan himself. While doing so, he proclaims a statement of certainty—*"I am baptized."*

Regardless of the unworthiness, doubt, or inadequacy you feel, the Gospel invites you to leave your old self behind and look at the Bible to see whom God chooses to work through. Everyone from Abraham and Moses to Peter and Paul brought with them baggage of many kinds. Paul himself reflects on this remarkable truth, saying:

I thank Him who has given me strength, Christ Jesus our Lord, because He judged me faithful, appointing me to His service, though formerly I was a blasphemer, persecutor, and insolent opponent. But I received mercy because I had acted ignorantly in unbelief, and the grace of our Lord overflowed for me with the faith and love that are in Christ Jesus. The saying is trustworthy and deserving of full acceptance, that Christ Jesus came into the world to save sinners, of whom I am the foremost. But I received mercy for this reason, that in me, as the foremost, Jesus Christ might display His perfect patience as an example to those who were to believe in Him for eternal life. (1 Timothy 1:12–16)

I just love that last part, and I hope you do too. I pray it gives you hope and quiets the whispers of the evil one, the lie that you don't measure up. Paul, the author of just about half of the New Testament, was once a persecutor of Christians. Yet he was chosen, redeemed, and forgiven as an example for you and me to know that if God's grace can work in him (and it did), it can be at work in us too. God invited Paul into community with Him. He invites you as well.

Regardless what you think about where you stand with God, know that Jesus made a space at His table just for you.

This is Jesus inviting you into community with Him, intentionally. This is His plan and His desire for you. You are not an accident. You are not a random collection of atoms that just happened to collide to make you. In fact, exactly the opposite is true:

> For You formed my inward parts; You knitted me together in my mother's womb. I praise You, for I am fearfully and wonderfully made. Wonderful are Your works; my soul knows it very well. My frame was not hidden from You, when I was being made in secret, intricately woven in the depths of the earth. (Psalm 139:13–15)

You were designed by God; You were created by God. You are fearfully and wonderfully made. Yes—you. You were not only created, but you were also redeemed; Jesus laid down His life for you. This was all to bring *you* into community with the triune God.

Is that awesome, or what?

Still not convinced? Consider this: well before Jesus asks His disciples to come to terms with who He is, He invites them simply to follow Him. "Follow Me" (Matthew 4:19) comes well before "Who do you say that I am?" (Matthew 16:15). This reveals a seismic truth: Jesus invites us to follow Him, to seek Him, and to be in community with Him, even if we haven't figured out everything about Him.

You likely have God questions; everybody does. Be assured that having questions does not disqualify you from following Jesus and from being in community with Him. In fact, well into Jesus' ministry, John the Baptist, the same guy who pointed to Jesus and called Him "the Lamb of God" (John 1:29), asked an honest question. Stuck in prison, with no hope for release and soon to be beheaded and martyred for his faith, John sends messengers to Jesus:

> Now when John heard in prison about the deeds of the Christ, he sent word by his disciples and said to Him, "Are You the one who is to come, or shall we look for another?" (Matthew 11:2–3)

You can understand why John asked. Prison and capital punishment probably were not the outcome he expected as a forerunner to the Messiah, so he wanted some reassurance from the Messiah Himself. John had questions. We have questions. Asking questions is healthy when they bring us to Jesus. Jesus responds to John with grace and truth, and He does the same for us:

> All things have been handed over to Me by My Father, and no one knows the Son except the Father, and no one knows the Father except the Son and anyone to whom the Son chooses to reveal Him. Come to Me, all who labor and are heavy laden, and I will give you rest. Take My yoke upon you, and learn from Me, for I am gentle and lowly in heart, and you will find rest for your souls. For My yoke is easy, and My burden is light. (Matthew 11:27–30)

It's not just the baggage of our questions that Jesus works with. In His last meal with His disciples before His crucifixion, Jesus knows that His betrayer, the one who would turn Him over to the Roman soldiers and the Jewish leadership, is sitting at the table with Him. Jesus' words:

> "He who has dipped his hand in the dish with Me will betray Me. The Son of Man goes as it is written of Him, but woe to that man by whom the Son of Man is betrayed! It would have been better for that man if he had not been born." Judas, who would betray Him, answered, "Is it I, Rabbi?" He said to him, "You have said so." (Matthew 26:23–25)

Imagine sitting down for a special holiday meal, and there with you is someone you know will turn his back on you. What would you do? If you're like me, you would likely confront him and remove him from your table. Not Jesus.

In fact, it's almost like Matthew, the author of this Gospel, wants to highlight the radical grace of this moment, because right after recording this exchange between Jesus and Judas, Matthew tells us what Jesus does next:

> Now as they were eating, Jesus took bread, and after blessing it broke it and gave it to the disciples, and said, "Take, eat; this is My body." And He took a cup, and when He had given thanks He gave it to them, saying, "Drink of it, all of you, for this is My blood of the covenant, which is poured out for many for the forgiveness of sins." (Matthew 26:26–28)

Take special note of the magnitude of this moment and what it means for us. Jesus welcomed this sinner to His last meal to receive His grace, knowing full well who that sinner was. And He still invites sinners, imperfect people, the inadequate, the nonreligious, the deniers, the questioners, the betrayers to come to Him, receive His grace, and find identity, belonging, and community. This includes you.

Like the paralyzed man who meets Jesus and is changed, we, too, are changed when we meet Jesus. In some ways, this change is instantaneous. Metaphorically, we were blind, and now we see; we were in darkness, and now we are in light. We call this *justification*—the once for all, life-altering work Jesus accomplishes for us on the cross. It changes us.

When Jesus brings us into community with Him, He also begins a wonderful work in us called *sanctification*—the steady process God works in us to align us more and more with Him and His will for us. As we remain in Him and remain in community with Him, this steady work continually makes us new. Read how Paul describes it:

> Not that I have already obtained this or am already perfect, but I press on to make it my own, because Christ Jesus has made me His own. Brothers, I do not consider that I have made it my own. But one thing I do: forgetting what lies behind and straining forward to what lies ahead, I press on toward the goal for the prize of the upward call of God in Christ Jesus. (Philippians 3:12–14)

Don't let the evil one whisper lies about your past that disqualify you from community with God. Disregard the untruth that because you are still a work in progress, you can't have identity and belonging in Him.

In fact, and this is where we turn in the next chapter, God's vision for His Church is that it be a place where people who are changed by God's grace, although still imperfect, receive His grace anew and together pursue life in Him. It's a truth that is often repeated and worth sharing again—the Church is not a museum for saints, but rather a hospital for sinners.

The Church is not a museum for saints, but rather a hospital for sinners.

And both of the following are true:

First, God deeply desires you to find identity, belonging, and community in Him. He's so intent upon it that He'll go to the cross, suffer, and die the death of a criminal so you might know life in Him.

Second, God deeply desires that you find identity, belonging, and community within the family He has created—His Church.

Life can do a number on us. Everyone has moments of doubt and wonder—*do I fit in?* But the certain word of Jesus Christ draws us to Himself—where we *do* fit in.

I close this chapter with a memory that highlights for me the distinctiveness of God's heart and posture toward me.

When I was in junior high school, I was an average clarinet player in the band. Our school was well regarded for its outstanding music program, and accordingly, the teachers were known to push their students toward excellence. Part of the narrative was that if a student ever tried to step away from band, great effort was made to talk him or her out of it.

After seventh grade, I didn't want to continue band. I had heard horror stories about telling the band teacher that you were done. But one day at the end of the year, I gathered all my courage and was prepared for the tough conversation. I practiced my monologue. I was equipped with a bevy of reasons and was determined to stand strong no matter what. After school, I headed to the music wing. Here is a transcript of the conversation:

Me: Hello. I don't think I am going to do band next year.

Band teacher: Okay. Leave your clarinet in the cabinet outside my office.

What happened? It's clear the band teacher had given up on me, and frankly I don't blame him. I didn't practice very often, I talked too much during rehearsals, and I didn't show a lot of promise for the future.

God is nothing like my old band teacher.

Regardless of your past and despite your present, even with your checkered history and uncertain future, God never gives up on you. Quite the opposite. He fervently and relentlessly desires that you find identity, belonging, and community in Him. From Paul to Judas, from the paralyzed man to you and me, He never ceases revealing His heart of grace, forgiveness, and patience toward us.

> The Lord is not slow to fulfill His promise as some count slowness, but is patient toward you, not wishing that any should perish, but that all should reach repentance. (2 Peter 3:9)

Questions to invite reflection and conversation

1. In which way have you experienced "the world beating up on you"—through comparison, the quest for achievement, or feelings of inadequacy?

2. How is the forgiveness Christ Jesus won for you especially meaningful for you? How does it change you?

3. What does it mean to you to find your sense of identity and belonging in Jesus Christ?

4. We defined sanctification as "the steady process God works in us to align us more and more with Him and His will for us." How do you sense His sanctifying work in your life? How is He shaping you and drawing you closer to Him and His will?

5. How does the lengthy history of God working through imperfect people bring you comfort?

CHAPTER 3

GOD'S VISION
FOR PEOPLE IN COMMUNITY

A few years back, I had an experience that you might identify with. Our oldest daughter began competitive swimming, and because this is something that neither my wife nor I had ever experienced, we had to learn a lot—and learn it quickly! It didn't take too long to figure out the rhythms of practices and what our daughter needed, but her first swim meet was an entirely different story.

I'm not sure I've ever felt more like an outsider. I thought everyone spent the day around the pool, watching, but that was not the case. Instead, swimmers and their families wait in the gym for their time to come, and then they are ushered first to "up next" waiting rooms, and then finally to the pool itself. I followed along and pretended like I knew what was going on, but inside I was clueless. People were asking me questions about heats and relays, which I had no idea how to answer. I felt like everyone except me knew what to do. When it came time to watch my daughter's race, I was standing in the wrong place. I had no concept how long the meet was going to last, when it would be over, or even if it went well.

Have you ever had an experience like that, one where you felt like an absolute outsider? material store ✓ produce

Church can feel like that for some people. While it's a place of comfort for those who are familiar with it, for others it can feel like that swim meet felt for me. While some of us are so familiar with its rhythms and practices, others may feel as though they've entered a foreign country. Although folks can follow along, inside they are feeling uncomfortable, afraid to make a mistake, and wondering if they are allowed to be there at all. Even though few if any are noticing, it feels to them like everyone is!

When Jesus Christ invites you into community with Him, He brings you simultaneously into a community with others. This community is called His Church. And regardless how you feel or whether you're not sure if you're supposed to sit or stand, sing or listen, you are not only *allowed* to be there, you are *supposed* to be there because Jesus shed His blood to make it so! Because Jesus has brought you into community with Him and with others, you become not just a member of His family (His Church), but you also become essential to the community.

This is the primary argument the New Testament makes about the Church, and it powerfully and winsomely uses the illustration of the human body to bring it home.

Advancements in technology and research on the human body give us a greater appreciation not only for its intricacy but also for the multitude of beautiful ways the parts and systems of the body work in concert. Check it out, and although it might be tempting to just skip past all this biology, I encourage you to take it slow and let the complexity of God's creation truly sink in:

> The human body contains trillions of cells, 78 different organs and more than 60,000 miles of blood vessels if you stretched them end-to-end. Incredibly, all of these cells, vessels and organs work together to keep you alive.
>
> Each organ belongs to one of ten human body systems. These body systems are interconnected and dependent upon one another to function. Your heart does not beat unless your brain and nervous system tell it to do so. Your skeletal system relies on the nutrients it gains from your digestive system to build strong, healthy bones. . . .
>
> Each individual body system works in conjunction with other body systems. The circulatory system is a good example of how body systems interact with each other. Your heart pumps blood through a complex network of blood vessels. When your blood circulates through your digestive system, for example, it picks up nutrients

your body absorbed from your last meal. Your blood also carries oxygen inhaled by the lungs. Your circulatory system delivers oxygen and nutrients to the other cells of your body then picks up any waste products created by these cells, including carbon dioxide, and delivers these waste products to the kidneys and lungs for disposal. Meanwhile, the circulatory system carries hormones from the endocrine system, and the immune system's white blood cells that fight off infection. . . .

Even seemingly unrelated body systems are connected. Your skeletal system relies on your urinary system to remove waste produced by bone cells; in return, the bones of your skeleton create structure that protects your bladder and other urinary system organs. Your circulatory system delivers oxygen-rich blood to your bones. Meanwhile, your bones are busy making new blood cells.

Working together, these systems maintain internal stability and balance, otherwise known as homeostasis.[5]

Two amazing truths strike me after reading that:

· First, this is God's design—how amazing! As the verse cited earlier proclaims, we are indeed "fearfully and wonderfully made" (Psalm 139:14).

· Second, God chose this—how the human body works together—as the primary means by which we understand His Church.

---

5   reverehealth.com/live-better/how-body-systems-connected/

Of all the visuals God could have chosen to help us grasp His vision for His Church, He intentionally chose the human body because we are familiar with it. We sometimes miss this, and culture's understanding of the Church misses it as well. Think for a moment about what "church" can be made out to be.

Sometimes, we define church only as a *place*. It's somewhere we go.

Sometimes, we define church only as an *experience*. We evaluate it like a movie and determine whether it is exciting and entertaining or emotionless and boring.

Sometimes, we define church only by its *leadership*. We've merged our feelings about church with our feelings about the pastor. If we like the pastor, we like the church. If the pastor fails, we feel burned by the church.

God's definition and vision for His Church, however, is thankfully broader than we might first realize, and this ought to give us great comfort (as we'll explore below). But now let's take a look at one place in the Bible that really brings this home. Be on the lookout for how the concept of *community* is woven into the text:

> For just as the body is one and has many members, and all the members of the body, though many, are one body, so it is with Christ. For in one Spirit we were all baptized into one body—Jews or Greeks, slaves or free—and all were made to drink of one Spirit.

For the body does not consist of one member but of many. If the foot should say, "Because I am not a hand, I do not belong to the body," that would not make it any less a part of the body. And if the ear should say, "Because I am not an eye, I do not belong to the body," that would not make it any less a part of the body. If the whole body were an eye, where would be the sense of hearing? If the whole body were an ear, where would be the sense of smell? But as it is, God arranged the members in the body, each one of them, as He chose. If all were a single member, where would the body be? As it is, there are many parts, yet one body. *Each part has a function.* The eye cannot say to the hand, "I have no need of you," nor again the head to the feet, "I have no need of you." On the contrary, the parts of the body that seem to be weaker are indispensable, and on those parts of the body that we think less honorable we bestow the greater honor, and our unpresentable parts are treated with greater modesty, which our more presentable parts do not require. But God has so composed the body, giving greater honor to the part that lacked it, that there may be no division in the body, but that the members may have the same care for one another. If one member suffers, all suffer together; if one member is honored, all rejoice together. (1 Corinthians 12:12–26)

I love how a person's past status, or even one's present status, does not disqualify him or her from being part of the Body. Whether Jew or Greek, slave or free, all are included.

I love how each part is equally celebrated and important. While the world loves to distinguish and rank based on perceived importance, this doesn't happen in God's family. Wow.

And I love how each part is designed to be in concert with one another. God's family is not a loose collection of individuals who occasionally are in the same place at the same time. Instead, they are a people woven together, and each of us is truly indispensable.

This is God's vision for His community, His Church.

God's family is . . . a people woven together, and each of us is truly indispensable.

Are you ready for the best part? Following this healthy and helpful description of His vision for His Church, our Lord wants to make sure you get this message loud and clear:

> Now you are the body of Christ and individually members of it. (1 Corinthians 12:27)

Let that sink in for a moment.

Even with all your imperfections, your inadequacies, your failures, God has made a place at the table for you with Him and desires that you be in community with all His other people. Your presence as a part of God's family matters.

A sometimes overlooked narrative from the Old Testament provides a relatable and memorable expression of this. Found in Exodus 35, this happens after Moses received the Ten Commandments. It's time for God's people to build a sacred space, and Moses, as a messenger of God, relays how each person is to contribute in his own way, how each contribution is a beautiful expression of worship, and how each contribution matters. The people hear this and respond accordingly. Check out the result. Observe how this was a powerful manifestation of being a community, a body working together:

> And they came, everyone whose heart stirred him, and everyone whose spirit moved him, and brought the Lord's contribution to be used for the tent of meeting, and for all its service, and for the holy garments. So they came, both men and women. All who were of a willing heart brought brooches and earrings and signet rings and armlets, all sorts of gold objects, every man dedicating an offering of gold to the Lord. And every one who possessed blue or purple or scarlet yarns or fine linen or goats' hair or tanned rams' skins or goatskins brought them. Everyone who could make a contribution of silver or bronze brought it as the Lord's contribution. And every one who possessed acacia wood of any use in the work brought it. And every skillful woman spun with her hands, and they all brought what they had spun in blue and purple and scarlet yarns and fine twined linen. All the women whose

hearts stirred them to use their skill spun the goats' hair. And the leaders brought onyx stones and stones to be set, for the ephod and for the breastpiece, and spices and oil for the light, and for the anointing oil, and for the fragrant incense. All the men and women, the people of Israel, whose heart moved them to bring anything for the work that the LORD had commanded by Moses to be done brought it as a freewill offering to the LORD. (Exodus 35:21–29)

Well before the New Testament brought to us the idea of the Church as a body, God's people were practicing it. Some brought garments and jewelry; others brought animal skins. Some brought their wood for woodworking; others brought their spinning skills. Each person contributed in his or her own way, and each contribution was significant and necessary.

This is still God's vision for His people. And we need one another more than ever before. The first chapter of this book reminds us of the cultural headwinds we face, resulting in a startling increase of isolation, loneliness, and anxiety. Unfortunately, the response is often tribalism, division, and divisiveness. Through His Church, our Lord invites us to find identity, belonging, and community in Him and with one another. By His work, we are brought into a community where each person is equally honored, valued, and needed.

Recently, a co-worker introduced me to "bouldering." No, I didn't go do it, but she told me about it. Bouldering is a form of rock climbing that is performed on small rock formations or artificial rock walls without the use of ropes or other safety equipment. What's neat about bouldering is that it is practiced in community. As you climb, you can reach points where you don't have another move. From your vantage point, there is no place to put a hand or a foot to continue your climb. But those below you, who have a different vantage point, help you see what you cannot, and with their help, you can advance.

What a perfect snapshot of the power and benefit of living in community. May this be what we experience in the Church!

Volunteering Service

Take a moment to think about memorable experiences you've had with groups of people. Perhaps it was a family trip, a team that succeeded, a project you shared with co-workers, or something good you were able to do within a group.

I think of football and baseball teams I was on while growing up that defied the odds and won games we weren't supposed to win. I think of a trip from my childhood home in upstate New York to the Grand Canyon and other national parks in the southwest United States that I took with four other family members, driving in and camping out of a minivan. I think of mission trips with church groups to Juarez, Mexico, to build a home in a week. Some of the most powerful experiences are shared experiences.

Very early in my ministry at the church where I presently serve, we entered a charity, coed, double elimination softball tournament in our town. We assembled a team that had never played together, and our expectations were low. We lost one of our first games, putting us in the loser's bracket and were one loss away from elimination. We expected to be home by lunch.

What happened next was a run for the ages—at least in our minds! We won six games in a row, winning the entire tournament. The next day in church, we were all so excited to see one another and share how sore we were—we were all feeling our age! Nearly ten years later, we still talk about that silly softball tournament. The power of shared experience!

From time to time, the funeral home in our town calls me to officiate a funeral. It happens when the person who has died doesn't have a pastor, for a host of reasons, but the family would like one to come and officiate a service. Not having a relationship with the family until this moment, and watching them process and mourn this death, is interesting to me to hear what stories are told about the person who died and how he or she is remembered. I noticed it early on, and subsequent funeral services have confirmed it—what is most often remembered, celebrated, and shared are moments families experienced together. It's not job promotions or career successes, homes

What is most often remembered, celebrated, and shared are moments families experienced together.

or vehicles acquired, but moments the family experienced together. The power of shared experience.

Early in the ministry of Moses, not long after the hand of God enabled the children of Israel to cross the Red Sea while fleeing the Egyptians, Moses is leading the Israelites in battle as they continue their journey to the Promised Land. The Amalekites attack, and God leads Moses to execute a plan. Community and a shared experience would be the centerpiece:

> Moses said to Joshua, "Choose for us men, and go out and fight with Amalek. Tomorrow I will stand on the top of the hill with the staff of God in my hand." So Joshua did as Moses told him, and fought with Amalek, while Moses, Aaron, and Hur went up to the top of the hill. Whenever Moses held up his hand, Israel prevailed, and whenever he lowered his hand, Amalek prevailed. But Moses' hands grew weary, so they took a stone and put it under him, and he sat on it, while Aaron and Hur held up his hands, one on one side, and the other on the other side. So his hands were steady until the going down of the sun. And Joshua overwhelmed Amalek and his people with the sword. (Exodus 17:9–13)

At first glance, it seems like a curious, almost trivial, means for God to lead His people to victory. Yet on a closer look, we see the richness of the message God is bringing home with this historical narrative.

First, hands in the air are hands that point to God, who reigns on high from heaven and is the source of any blessing or victory. Moses keeping his hands in the air would be a powerful visual reminder to all who fought, both with the Israelites and against them, of who was fighting with them and for them. This is how you are winning—alignment with God! This is still true for us today and a reality we do well to keep before us.

Second, this is a victory they would win in community. Moses couldn't do it alone; he would get tired, and he would need help. Aaron and Hur would play an important role in the victory. They were meant to be in community.

"Moses . . . grew weary." Do you ever grow weary? Even if you can't think of a specific instance, know that you will grow tired and weary, and you will need help. All that life throws at us can indeed do a number on us; we'll need the help of other people. Other people around us will experience the same. We'll need to hold up one another—it's how God designed His Church to be. And how profound are the riches of growing and learning and being in community!

Jesus Himself knew this and put it into practice. We see this in the only story we have of Jesus between His birth narrative and the launch of His public ministry. And although it seems like a simple family story, Luke uses precious real estate in His Gospel to tell this story because it reveals the heart of Jesus for living in community, beginning with Himself.

In chapter 2, Luke describes the pilgrimage twelve-year-old Jesus and His family took to Jerusalem for the Passover, an annual occurrence. After celebrating the Passover, it's time to head home, and Jesus' family begins the days-long journey back to Nazareth. One day into their trip, Joseph and Mary, who assumed Jesus was within the large caravan of people, realize that He is not. I'm guessing chaos and panic ensued.

They begin the journey back to Jerusalem and are frantically looking for Him. Take a look at not only where they find Him but also at what He is doing:

> After three days they found Him in the temple, sitting among the teachers, listening to them and asking them questions. And all who heard Him were amazed at His understanding and His answers. And when His parents saw Him, they were astonished. And His mother said to Him, "Son, why have You treated us so? Behold, Your father and I have been searching for You in great distress." And He said to them, "Why were you looking for Me? Did you not know that I must be in My Father's house?" And they did not understand the saying that He spoke to them. And He went down with them and came to Nazareth and was submissive to them. And His mother treasured up all these things in her heart.
>
> And Jesus increased in wisdom and in stature and in favor with God and man. (Luke 2:46–52)

We sometimes think of Jesus as a finished product from the very beginning. The reality, Scripture tells us, is that He was growing, maturing, that He "increased in wisdom and in stature . . . with God and man." How did He do this? By being in His Father's house, sitting, listening, and asking questions. Practicing community.

I believe there is a lot more room in our culture for sitting, listening, and asking questions. We live in a culture that seems to thrive on telling and yelling. Everyone has an opinion on everything. Yet here Jesus models for us that we grow and increase in wisdom and in stature with God and man by sitting, listening, and asking questions.

There is a lot more room in our culture for sitting, listening, and asking questions.

One of my favorite parts of being a pastor is visiting our homebound folks, who, for various reasons, aren't able to come to worship very often. So I bring them God's Word and the Lord's Supper. I am blessed by doing so, because not only do I get to deliver God's gifts to God's people, but I also do a great deal of sitting, listening, and asking questions.

Recently I visited Bernie, a ninety-four-year-old woman with the spirit and determination of someone decades younger. We talked about life leading up to and during World War II; how blessed I was to hear this firsthand account! I asked her if she followed today's culture and politics.

She made a few comments, shared a few observations, and then concluded with this gem: *"Everyone needs to be kinder to one another."* Bernie nailed it.

From the Israelites building the tabernacle to Moses, Aaron, and Hur, and from Jesus to Bernie, the message is clear. God has wired His people to live in community with one another, to share the same compassion and mercy—the kindness—that Christ shows us. And those who choose to live embracing this gift will experience abundant blessings.

The local church is at its best when it puts this into practice; it is at its best when it makes a place at the table for all of God's people. The Church is at its best when it forsakes the artificial barriers the world puts up to divide us and instead celebrates the unity we truly have as children of God.

This attitude of kindness is one of the things I love about the church I presently serve. While not perfect, we have a track record, by God's grace and through the working of His Holy Spirit, of welcoming people with open arms, regardless of their background, economic status, political leanings, or any other human dividing wall. On more than a few Sundays, I've seen someone in our faith family who earned a doctorate in economics worshiping a few feet away from one of our food pantry clients.

If you think about it, the Church is probably one of the last places where something like this happens. Here's another example: if it weren't for being a part of our congregation, my children would have limited contact with senior citizens. At school, in sports and activities, and in our neighborhood, which is comprised predominately of families, they rarely interact with seniors. Yet because our church facilitates it, they see, talk with, and serve with this generation regularly.

Society and technology divide and segment us more and more. However, to be faithful to God's call and vision, the Church must be different. The Word of God ensures that you know that there is indeed a space and a place for you within the community He has created:

> For in Christ Jesus you are all sons of God, through faith. For as many of you as were baptized into Christ have put on Christ. There is neither Jew nor Greek, there is neither slave nor free, there is no male and female, for you are all one in Christ Jesus. And if you are Christ's, then you are Abraham's offspring, heirs according to promise. (Galatians 3:26–29)

In a world where loneliness, division, and tribalism dominate, Christ offers identity, belonging, and community with Him. And through the water and the Word of Baptism, He brings you into His family, the Church, where you have an essential role, receiving and giving care and enjoying the blessings of shared experience. This is God's plan for His people, His Church. And you are a significant part of it.

Have you ever stubbed your toe really badly? Isn't it remarkable how pain to such a tiny, often forgotten extremity can cause such anguish? When you strike your little toe on a chair or a table, your whole body bends over, you grimace and grab that toe. Your attention is fully on that little extremity. It's just a toe, but the whole body is impacted.

> If one member suffers, all suffer together; if one member is honored, all rejoice together. Now you are the body of Christ and individually members of it. (1 Corinthians 12:26–27)

God's vision for His people, His Church, is that we might be similarly aligned. May it be so.

Questions to invite reflection and conversation

1. Have you had an experience where you felt like an outsider? How did it feel?

2. Which element of the Bible's use of body imagery to describe the Church is most meaningful for you? Why?

3. Have you ever had a powerful group experience? Why do you think it was so impactful?

4. Do you ever find yourself growing weary? Who are the people who "hold up your hands"?

5. Where and with whom might you find yourself sitting, listening, and asking questions as Jesus does in Luke 2?

CHAPTER 4

PRACTICING AND LIVING IN COMMUNITY

Imagine that you are given the opportunity to host Jesus in your home. Would you be prepared? I'm guessing there are probably some home projects you would like to finish in order to get everything all ready for your important guest. Now fast-forward to the moment Jesus is actually *in* your home. You would do everything you could to make Him feel honored, wouldn't you? *"Honey, let's break out the good china!"*

The Bible records a home visit Jesus made to two people He loved dearly, Mary and Martha. Yet during the visit, they respond quite differently to Jesus' presence:

> Now as they went on their way, Jesus entered a village. And a woman named Martha welcomed Him into her house. And she had a sister called Mary, who sat at the Lord's feet and listened to His teaching. But Martha was distracted with much serving. And she went up to Him and said, "Lord, do You not care that my sister has left me to serve alone? Tell her then to help me." But the Lord answered her, "Martha, Martha, you are anxious and troubled about many things, but one thing is necessary. Mary has chosen the good

portion, which will not be taken away from her." (Luke 10:38–42)

I've heard my fair share of sermons on this exchange, and some criticize what Martha is doing. The takeaway is *"Don't be like Martha, all busy; rather be like Mary, who sits and listens to Jesus."* The subtle message is that Martha is bad while Mary is good, so be like Mary.

In reality, what Martha is doing here for Jesus is beautiful! She was ensuring that Jesus received the best hospitality, that He was honored and made comfortable. It could be that cooking for Jesus was her own act of love and worship. What a beautiful thing!

What she does is good, and Jesus never scolds her for it. But He does invite her to enjoy something better—resting and being in His presence, finding community with Him and the others among them.

In a similar way for us, there is so much good among us. Just like for Martha, there is a rich abundance of blessings and opportunities before us, from our families, to our vocations, to serving—there is so much good before us. Yet to echo Jesus, don't let something good get in the way of something better. Don't let good works get in the way of resting and being in His presence,

There is a rich abundance of blessings and opportunities before us.

finding community with Him and others with whom He has richly blessed us.

Finding identity and belonging and living in community with Jesus and His Church are essential to our life as His people. In this final chapter, we focus on putting into practice what we've talked about. We celebrate the fact that in Christ Jesus, we have identity, belonging, and community—thanks be to God. This is His work and gift to us. And in acts of grace upon grace, we are grafted into His family, His Body, the Church, to find a beautiful expression of community with one another.

But what will it look like to put this into practice?

As you've likely realized, living in community doesn't come naturally. As our culture drifts steadily toward hyper-individualism and its opposite, tribalism, drawing to community will feel increasingly like trying to walk up a down escalator. We'll have to fight for it—but it's worth it! Putting this into practice will take some intentional steps, and it will take practicing them with consistency. Along the way, you'll be tempted to give up, but the benefits of living in community are a rich reward. Jesus promises that pursuing life with Him and in Him and in community with others is blessed and results in abundant life:

> The thief comes only to steal and kill and destroy. I came that they may have life and have it abundantly. (John 10:10)

Quick disclaimer before we dive in—I'll be the first to admit that I'm a work in progress. The essential practices I describe here are not so much what I've accomplished but what I'm in the process of discovering. I'll point out how I've fallen short yet how the Lord continues to shape me. Well-known columnist and author David Brooks remarked, "I want to write my way to a better life."[6] Well said. I've seen the power of putting these into practice, and more important than my endorsement, the Bible confirms these.

Essential Practice 1 —
The Rhythm of Regular Worship

Across America, the trend is clear—the number of people attending a weekly worship service is on a steep and steady decline. In the last two decades, the number of people who are members of congregations has dropped 20 percent[7]—a sharp decrease after being consistent for generations. Meanwhile, the number of people whom researchers call the "nones," those declaring no religious affiliation at all, is at almost a quarter of the population and rising.[8] From my own experience as a pastor, there are fewer people who are

6   www.aspenideas.org/sessions/the-second-mountain-the-quest-for-a-moral-life

7   news.gallup.com/poll/248837/church-membership-down-sharply-past-two-decades.aspx

8   www.pewresearch.org/fact-tank/2015/05/13/a-closer-look-at-americas-rapidly-growing-religious-nones/

a part of a faith community, who are engaged and connected with it, and who attend worship services. When I was growing up, it seemed like <u>families</u> that belonged to a congregation worshiped about fifty Sundays a year. <u>Today,</u> it seems to me like it is only <u>once a month.</u> The reason I believe this is complicated, but <u>we need the rhythm of regular worship services more now than ever.</u>

People who study this stuff estimate that you and I receive up to ten thousand messages a day[9] through various media. We are inundated with input from people, retailers, political parties, organizations, entertainment, employers, services trying to tell us something, sell us something, scare us, convince us, or get us to do something. This results in our feeling stretched and pulled in a hundred directions. Can you identify? Think for a moment—<u>how many of these messages seek to draw you closer to the Lord and His promises</u> in Christ Jesus? <u>How many align with biblical values and encourage you to a life in Christ?</u> I'm guessing a small percentage.

This is why in an increasingly secular world, <u>we need to</u> listen to the Lord. In the rhythm of <u>regular worship, we receive a needed break</u> and <u>rest from all that pulls us,</u> a rest that helps us refocus on the life "which is truly life" (1 Timothy 6:19).

Gloom + doom of politics bring me closer to the truth of God's Word

9   www.forbes.com/sites/forbesagencycouncil/2017/08/25/finding-brand-success-in-the-digital-world/

This was the Lord's vision for His people from the very beginning. He created the world in six twenty-four-hour days, and on the seventh day, He rested. And just to be clear—God didn't rest because He was tired! He rested to establish a rhythm for us to follow. If God, who holds His whole creation in His hand, can cease work and rest, we can too.

This dedicated time is so important to God that He makes it the third of His Ten Commandments:

> Remember the Sabbath day, to keep it holy. Six days you shall labor, and do all your work, but the seventh day is a Sabbath to the LORD your God. On it you shall not do any work, you, or your son, or your daughter, your male servant, or your female servant, or your livestock, or the sojourner who is within your gates. For in six days the LORD made heaven and earth, the sea, and all that is in them, and rested on the seventh day. Therefore the LORD blessed the Sabbath day and made it holy. (Exodus 20:8–11)

Interestingly enough, *Sabbath* actually means "stop." God knew we would be tempted to work, labor, produce, and strive to achieve, get ahead, accumulate more. Knowing this about human nature, God builds in a day for us to stop, rest, recharge, and be reminded of where we find identity, belonging, and community.

As a part of our understanding of Sabbath, Lutherans have a somewhat unique theology of worship. Foundationally, we understand worship as God's work, as God serving us with His gifts. Worship is not about our giving anything to God; rather, we know worship as God delivering to us His abundant gifts—grace, mercy, peace, forgiveness, wisdom, strength, to name a few. We desperately need these gifts, so it is essential that we establish a rhythm to receive them regularly.

In a world wired to celebrate achievement and the system of working and earning, it's tempting to think of worship like that. In this scheme, worship becomes what we do to earn or maintain God's favor. It becomes about us showing up for God, giving God the praise He is due or acquiring increased head knowledge about God.

Worship, however, is better understood as God inviting us out of this mentality and into something entirely different. Worship is God delivering His gifts to His people, who simply come with open ears, mouths, and hearts to receive them.

Worship is God delivering His gifts to His people.

Think about our posture when we celebrate and receive the Lord's Supper. We come as beggars, with nothing to offer God in exchange for all He is giving to us. We come with hands extended, mouths open, and sometimes we even take on the ultimate stance of need—we kneel.

The Book of Hebrews nails this understanding of worship as rest and gift:

So then, there remains a Sabbath rest for the people of God, for whoever has entered God's rest has also rested from his works as God did from His. Let us therefore strike to enter that rest, so that no one may fall by the same sort of disobedience. (Hebrews 4:9–11)

Take special note of the call to "strive to enter that rest." The Lord calls us to this because He knows how much we need it. Establishing and practicing a rhythm of regular worship takes us back to that identity, belonging, and community Jesus established for us.

Regular worship is part of my vocation as a pastor. Leading public worship services is a part of my week. From Sunday morning worship, to midweek and special services, to weddings and funerals, I am regularly in worship.

Yet I confess, I don't always feel like it. Sometimes, my mind is in a hundred different places as I begin worship. Sometimes, something urgent or important is before me, and it's hard to think about anything else as I begin worship. Not too long ago, I woke up on a Sunday morning to discover that our furnace had broken overnight. Ugh. As I drove to church that morning, prepared for worship, and began the service, many questions raced through my head. Could it be fixed? Who should we call? How long can a house function in the winter without a furnace? If it can't be fixed, how much will a new one cost?

If worship weren't part of my job, I probably would have stayed home to tackle the issue. But then I would have missed what God did to me and for me, what He worked in me that Sunday morning.

Being in worship that Sunday—connecting with God's people, singing, hearing His Word, and receiving His body and blood—centered me, grounded me, and changed me. God's peace enveloped me. I was reminded that God's got this. I began to be thankful that it didn't happen when we were out of town; rather, it happened when we were home and could handle it before anything else bad happened. I remembered to trust Him. Worship was where I needed to be, especially because I had a hundred things on my mind.

Worship is where God does necessary work in my life. This is not true only for me. It's true for you too.

Sometimes, during worship, I look around to gauge the mood and vibe of the sanctuary. I see who is present, how people seem, and the like. Sometimes, I pray—thanking God for these moments and asking Him to be at work among us. You see, even the pastor's mind wanders during worship from time to time.

Worship is where God does necessary work in my life.

What I think about the most is this—those among us choose to be present because they know they need it. You need it. During weeks that have you scurrying and worrying, you get to set aside an hour to put all that aside. You get to be present in a place where nothing is asked of you. God does the work of worship. He comes to you with His gifts, and you receive, give thanks, and respond.

In Matthew 11:28–29, Jesus shares these words:

> Come to Me, all who labor and are heavy laden, and I will give you rest. Take My yoke upon you, and learn from Me, for I am gentle and lowly in heart, and you will find rest for your souls.

A few thoughts here.

- First, Jesus invites us to come to Him. Don't go elsewhere, as tempting as it is. Candy Crush or a Netflix binge might take you away, but it will not fill you up with what you need. Genuine peace is found only in Jesus Christ.

- Second, when we come to Him, He gives us the rest we desperately need. Not a physical sleep-type rest, but a mental "you don't need to do anything here" kind of rest, a spiritual recharging kind of rest. We need this rest.

- Finally, rejoice that with Jesus, there is no burden to perform or achieve. We come as flawed, imperfect, incomplete people. Jesus takes the burden of achievement from us by being perfectly obedient to God's Law and by fulfilling all righteousness (see Matthew 3:15).

First-century Jewish culture had a host of different schools of thought and rabbis to teach them. When you followed a specific rabbi, you were taking his yoke upon yourself. This included following his commands and interpretations of Judaism. In the Divine Service, however, Jesus invites us to follow Him and to take on His yoke of gentleness and humility rather than performance or achievement. Here it is promised, "you will find rest for your souls."

When we're in worship, we are *with* God. He is present in His Word. He is present in the Sacrament of the Holy Supper.

Since they were written, the words of Psalm 23 have brought great comfort to God's people. To give you a moment of needed rest, right now, I invite you to hear them anew, to receive them in light of how we've been speaking of worship, Sabbath, and rest. You might be tempted to skim the psalm because it's familiar, but allow yourself a moment to read the words slowly and to be refreshed:

> The LORD is my shepherd; I shall not want.
>   He makes me lie down in green pastures.
> He leads me beside still waters.
>   He restores my soul.
> He leads me in paths of righteousness
>   for His name's sake.
> Even though I walk through the valley of the shadow of death,

I will fear no evil,
for You are with me;
    Your rod and Your staff,
    they comfort me.
You prepare a table before me
    in the presence of my enemies;
You anoint my head with oil;
    my cup overflows.
Surely goodness and mercy shall follow me
    all the days of my life,
and I shall dwell in the house of the Lord
    forever.

What beautifully rich worship language is here. No wonder this psalm has been a blessing to so many throughout the generations. Here are a few elements to pay special attention to:

> *"The Lord is my shepherd."* Not might be, not could be, He *is.* And because He is this for us, there is a shift in us.

> *"I shall not want."* In a culture that demands so much, in a culture of striving and discontent, those who find identity, belonging, and community in Christ shall *not* want. Wow.

> *"He makes me lie down."* We won't instinctively know to do it, so He tells us how. This is the Third

Commandment with its call to worship and rest. He leads us not only to lie down but to lie down in the green pastures of His presence.

The world and all that it offers is loud and choppy, but God leads His people to still waters, and here we are truly restored.

Life will still be treacherous. Sometimes, we'll feel like we're walking through the valley of the shadow of death. But in these times, we are invited to fear not. Why? Because we know He is with us. He makes a space and a place at His Table for us where blessings overflow. All this is not just a temporal reality, but a forever, eternal dwelling with the Lord in His house.

Jesus invites you into this. The rhythm of regular worship takes you here. Here you are reminded of your identity. Sometimes it feels like the world has us on a leash and drags us here and there. Ever feel pulled in a hundred directions or stretched like Gumby? The rhythm of regular worship reminds you who you are and whose you are. It reframes your knowledge of identity, belonging, and community. Regularly receiving the Word of God, the Lord's Supper, and His shepherding of us to these green pastures and still waters is essential to our lives.

> *The rhythm of regular worship reminds you who you are and whose you are.*

Not long ago, I was preaching about rest and Sabbath and honoring what is truly important. During my message, a mom received a text from her son's baseball coach. Although the team didn't have scheduled practice that afternoon, the coach was gathering players for extra batting practice. The mom's first instinct was to respond that her son would be there. In the moment, and without thinking through the implications of it, her initial response was always to say yes to the call of youth sports. Yet because she was in worship and was being reminded of the value of Sabbath and rest and time together as a family, she texted, *"Sorry, can't make it today. It's family day in our home."* That warm spring afternoon was instead dedicated to family time because the Word of the Lord reminded them of the value of taking time out to worship and to rest. The next Sunday, the mom shared this story with me, and she was still smiling about it.

The answer to a world experiencing rapidly increasing anxiety is not "don't be anxious." When someone says don't worry, you usually worry even more! Instead, you are invited into this Church, this Body of Christ, this family, this community—a place of total unconditional acceptance. For an hour or two a week, nothing is demanded of you; you don't need to perform or achieve. Instead, you can rest, receive, and be refreshed.

Our family loves to vacation in Arcadia, Michigan, tucked in the northwest part of the Lower Peninsula and perfectly placed on the beautiful shores of Lake Michigan. Trinity Lutheran Church in downtown Arcadia is our place of worship when we are there. The whole community is a bit of a throwback to what communities once were, and Trinity's sanctuary is no different. The Lord's Supper is celebrated around a Communion rail, where a dozen or so at a time come, kneel, and together receive. When the church is full, this takes time. But it is worth it. These are God's people, in community, coming to receive God's gifts for them. This is the Church, celebrating together an essential practice of living in community with God and with one another—the rhythm of regular worship service.

Essential Practice 2 — Christian Relationships

It's a truth so ingrained into how we understand the New Testament that I'm afraid we've lost sight of how powerful it truly is: upon launching His public ministry, Jesus is almost constantly living with, traveling with, teaching with, and in community with His disciples. In fact, the writers of the Gospels draw attention to the moments Jesus actually seeks solitude. Moments such as this:

> And rising very early in the morning, while it was still dark, He departed and went out to a desolate place, and there He prayed. (Mark 1:35)

Jesus takes these times of solitude and prayer as breaks from His norm—life in community with His disciples. His life with them included navigating their questions, insecurities, fears, and the like. Jesus had much to deal with, relationally. In fact, take a look at this scene to get a sense for all that Jesus navigated:

> And they [the disciples] were on the road, going up to Jerusalem, and Jesus was walking ahead of them. And they were amazed, and those who followed were afraid. And taking the twelve again, He began to tell them what was to happen to Him, saying, "See, we are going up to Jerusalem, and the Son of Man will be delivered over to the chief priests and the scribes, and they will condemn Him to death and deliver Him over to the Gentiles. And they will mock Him and spit on Him, and flog Him and kill Him. And after three days He will rise." (Mark 10:32–34)

So we have Jesus leading the way, heading toward Jerusalem and His Passion, followed closely by His disciples, who are in awe of Jesus. Behind them is still another group, numbering much more than twelve, who are afraid. With knowledge of His looming crucifixion, Jesus pulls the Twelve aside and gives them clear warning of what is soon to come. All that was ahead of Jesus was enough to consume His thoughts and prayers. But in this moment, observing all who are with Him, Jesus thinks of His relationships, His community, and how this would impact His followers. He seeks to prepare them.

Again, Jesus could have done His ministry alone. His ministry of teaching, healing, resurrecting, and so much more didn't need co-laborers. God the Son was plenty capable. Yet He calls people to follow Him, and in doing so, He invites them to find community with one another and with Him. He elects to draw people alongside Him—to walk where He walks, to sit at His feet, to observe and participate in His ministry—because He knew that the best way to mentor those who after His ascension would be the leaders of the Early Church was to invite them into community with Him. Jesus lived in community, with intentionality.

Jesus modeled for us, as the disciples did as well, the second essential practice of living in community—Christian relationships.

From the outset of His ministry, soon after His Baptism by John and His victory over temptation by Satan, Jesus called twelve men, the disciples, to follow Him. They left everything behind to go where He went, and together they formed a community. The disciples individually formed their own relationships with Him, and they formed relationships with one another as well. They broke off in pairs when Jesus sent them out, likely deepening the bond with at least one other person. Interestingly enough, modern research on team and small-group dynamics confirms the power of groups that number around twelve because this size fosters the formation of different levels of relationship within the same community.

Jesus models this as well. While Jesus had His Twelve, He also had His "Three." Jesus took Peter, James, and John to places He did not take the others. For example, in Luke 8, Jesus was on the way to the home of a synagogue ruler named Jairus, whose daughter had fallen gravely ill. While Jairus was leading them to his home, he received a message that his daughter had died. Brokenhearted, he called off the journey. But Jesus had other plans. Note who was invited to witness this moment:

> While He was still speaking, someone from the ruler's house came and said, "Your daughter is dead; do not trouble the Teacher any more." But Jesus on hearing this answered him, "Do not fear; only believe, and she will be well." And when He came to the house, He allowed no one to enter with Him, except Peter and John and James, and the father and mother of the child. And all were weeping and mourning for her, but He said, "Do not weep, for she is not dead but sleeping." And they laughed at Him, knowing that she was dead. But taking her by the hand He called, saying, "Child, arise." And her spirit returned, and she got up at once. And He directed that something should be given her to eat. (Luke 8:49–55)

Similarly, at the transfiguration of Jesus:

> And after six days Jesus took with Him Peter and James, and John his brother, and led them up a high mountain by themselves. And He was transfigured before them, and His face shone like the sun, and His clothes became white as light. (Matthew 17:1–2)

Finally, in Jesus' hour of great need, He called upon the same three:

> Then Jesus went with them to a place called Gethsemane, and He said to His disciples, "Sit here, while I go over there and pray." And taking with Him Peter and the two sons of Zebedee, He began to be sorrowful and troubled. Then He said to them, "My soul is very sorrowful, even to death; remain here, and watch with Me." (Matthew 26:36–38)

What does this reveal? There is need for community in a larger circle, and there is also a need for tight bonds with a few. Deep, unique, and intentional relationships are essential to practicing and living in Christian community.

The Bible puts it this way: "Iron sharpens iron, and one man sharpens another" (Proverbs 27:17). This means that one iron blade is used to sharpen another blade, which prepares both to fulfill their functions. Over time, blades used alone would become dull and ineffective. Another blade is necessary to sharpen it; it is impossible for one blade to get sharper without the aid and presence of the other. The best part? In the act of sharpening the dull blade, both blades become sharper.

What a powerful vision for the Christian in relationship!

I've gone through ministry seasons when I didn't have this understanding. I've focused on tasks at hand, neglecting the sharpening that others in the faith have for me and perhaps the sharpening I could do for others. In those seasons, I felt isolation and loneliness. I felt dull.

One component of God's manifold grace in my life comes in the form of two local pastors who are essential to me. We meet regularly, and through God's Holy Spirit, Proverbs 27:17 happens. Because we have built trust over years spent together, we have permission to speak into one another's lives, and no question is out-of-bounds. There are times when I am with them that I discover something about myself—thought processes, attitudes, or actions that I didn't recognize until they "sharpened" it out of me. Thanks be to God.

Interestingly, just as Jesus had His Twelve and His Three, there is a different dynamic with two of us than there is with three of us. With one of the other pastors, we serve as each other's accountability partner. In this relationship, we have a deeper understanding of the needs, challenges, and struggles of the other. We commit to regular prayer for each other, and there is a regular checking in with each other between meetings. In this way, iron is sharpened.

With both of my accountability partners and with the three of us brothers in the Lord, this biblical truth is equally realized: "Bear one another's burdens, and so fulfill the law of Christ" (Galatians 6:2).

Because the New Testament was originally written in Greek, sometimes we get a richer sense of meaning when we see which Greek words were used. The Greek word used here for "bear" is *bastazo*, and most often it is used to describe a physical carrying of something. The gift God has given us of Christian relationships is that we in essence "carry" struggles and challenges for one another. Deep, unique, and intentional relationships are essential to practicing and living in Christian community.

Deep, unique, and intentional relationships are essential to practicing and living in Christian community.

Some five hundred years ago, Martin Luther recognized the essential value of this gift. In what is sometimes referred to as Luther's theological last will and testament, the Smalcald Articles, he writes, "We will now return to the Gospel, which not merely in one way gives us counsel and aid against sin; for God is superabundantly rich [and liberal] in His grace [and goodness]." Here, Luther points out the manifold ways God delivers His grace to His people. After discussing the Means of Grace, the Word, Baptism, and the Lord's Supper, Luther refers to God's grace delivered through "the mutual conversation and consolation of brethren."[10] Luther recognized that within Christian friendships, God's grace is delivered to one another, iron sharpens iron, and burdens are carried.

In His earthly ministry, Jesus promises that this is true, chiefly because when His people gather in His name, a special gift is among them:

> Again I say to you, if two of you agree on earth about anything they ask, it will be done for them by My Father in heaven. For where two or three are gathered in My name, there am I among them. (Matthew 18:19–20)

A quick word is in order here regarding this topic and men. I struggled with headlining this subsection "Christian Relationships" out of fear that even the word *relationships* would cause some in the male species to tune out. The "R" word can be uncomfortable for men to talk about. *Not nurterers by nature.*

But the reality is this—while sometimes women form relationships with ease, the opposite can be true for men. There is a host of reasons why, but at the core, I believe that the elements of building deep, unique, and intentional relationships simply come easier for women.

Our church of a few hundred has some seventy-five women who attend an annual retreat; meanwhile, our men's group can fit at a few tables.

men don't want to expose themselves

10   bookofconcord.org/smalcald.php#gospel

Whereas women confide in other women.

Because of this, it's doubly important that men pay attention to this, pursue this, pray for this, and not give up on this. Men benefit from deep, unique, and intentional relationships. Although they might wear it well or stuff it down, men can fall into patterns of loneliness and isolation and struggle with issues of identity and belonging. God has wired each of us, men and women alike, to need community and Christian relationships.

God has wired each of us, men and women alike, to need community and Christian relationships.

Some time ago, I got some news I wasn't expecting. It was a rejection of sorts, and I was blindsided by it. And I was hurt. I wallowed for about forty-five minutes or so, and the evil one loved it. I felt dejected, ineffective, and doubt ran wild.

Then I texted four friends. I shared with them a brief summary of what happened and how I was feeling. What happened next was awesome and was the Lord's provision for me. My phone was a channel for good, as these friends shared words of encouragement with me via text. I felt affirmed, valued, and hopeful. My community blessed me and changed me. Deep, unique, and intentional relationships are essential to practicing and living in Christian community.

When I was growing up, my father worked in financial accounting. In the months of January through March, he was very busy, working longer hours than usual at the office and even working at home. I specifically remember a computer his company allowed him to bring home during these busy seasons. This was circa 1985. The computer was in a large, white, hard-shell plastic case; it was heavy. I distinctly remember it because my dad allowed me to play on it after he was done with his work. Reflecting on that now, I'm a bit surprised by that parenting decision. (Haha!)

One Saturday, while he was doing another project at home, I didn't have the patience to wait for his permission to use the computer. I carried the heavy computer upstairs to my room, one stair at a time. It was heavy, especially for a five-year-old.

Sometime after I set it up, my dad found me at his keyboard. Needless to say, he was very surprised. Yet here's what I specifically remember—he didn't so much take on a scolding posture as a "why didn't you just ask?" posture. As if to say, "I'm allowing you to do this. It's a gift and a treasure; just please ask for help."

In a similar way, God has designed us to live, and thrive, in Christian relationships. Some one hundred times, the New Testament uses "one another" language, highlighting the unique role we have in relationship with one another and in the Christian community. One hundred times! Here is one of my favorites:

Let love be genuine. Abhor what is evil; hold fast to what is good. Love one another with brotherly affection. Outdo one another in showing honor. Do not be slothful in zeal, be fervent in spirit, serve the Lord. Rejoice in hope, be patient in tribulation, be constant in prayer. Contribute to the needs of the saints and seek to show hospitality. (Romans 12:9–13)

What a precious and treasured gift the Lord gives us in Christian relationships!

Essential Practice 3 — Serving Together

"I'm not doing it; *you* do it!"

These are words you'd expect to hear from a moody teenager. But would you believe me if I told you these were basically the words Jesus once said to His disciples? The narrative is familiar to many, but it's easy to overlook Jesus' somewhat surprising response to His disciples and the message behind it. Take a look:

Now when Jesus heard this, He withdrew from there in a boat to a desolate place by Himself. But when the crowds heard it, they followed Him on foot from the towns. When He went ashore He saw a great crowd, and He had compassion on them and healed their sick. Now when it was evening, the disciples came to Him and said, "This is a desolate place, and the day is now over; send the crowds away to go into the villages and buy food for themselves." But Jesus said, "They

need not go away; **you give them something to eat**."
They said to Him, "We have only five loaves here and
two fish." And He said, "Bring them here to Me." Then
He ordered the crowds to sit down on the grass, and
taking the five loaves and the two fish, He looked up to
heaven and said a blessing. Then He broke the loaves
and gave them to the disciples, and the disciples gave
them to the crowds. And they all ate and were satis-
fied. And they took up twelve baskets full of the broken
pieces left over. And those who ate were about five
thousand men, besides women and children. (Matthew
14:13–21, emphasis added)

Could Jesus have performed this entire miracle by
Himself, with no help from His disciples? Of course. But by
Jesus choosing to include them, Jesus reveals that He wanted His
disciples to discover the power, blessings, and benefits of
being hands on with Him in the work of God. He wanted them
to know the abundant blessings of serving together.

I wonder what it was like for the disciples after this
moment. Perhaps they had the mood of the locker room of
the winning team after the Super Bowl—lots of jubilation, high
fives, and the feeling of mission accomplished. Or perhaps
they were left stunned and in awe of what they had just been
a part of.

Either way, they lived through something profound and
in doing so experienced the third essential practice of living
in community—the power of serving together. God blesses

these experiences and leverages them to grow His people in beautiful ways.

In addition to volunteering and serving in her church, my mom is also a volunteer with the historical association in her town. I can tell she really likes serving with this group—she likes history, and she likes preserving it for younger generations. But most of all, I think she loves the people she serves with. When she meets with her partner to prepare for future classroom presentations, their conversations include not only the task at hand but also life updates and care for each other. And fairly often, their time together is extended with a meal! She loves serving alongside her friend.

At first glance, it might be easy to dismiss the significance of this reality as commonsense and, perhaps, commonplace. Yet when I reflect on both what best shapes and forms Christian community and what keeps people living in community, I keep coming back to the power of people serving together. Simply put, community is best realized among people who serve together.

Community is best realized among people who serve together.

Karen and Lynda are two women who have been tight for as long as I've known them, and it turns out they've been tight much longer than that. They are probably as close of friends as I know, and watching them look out for each other and provide self-sacrificial care for each other is inspiring. Curious about their friendship, I asked them how they became such good friends. Ready for the answer? "We taught Sunday School together a *long* time ago!" The power of serving together.

The story of Moses and Aaron is a wonderful reminder of the personal impact of serving together. You might remember that God called Moses to a critically important role—to lead God's people out of slavery in Egypt and into the Promised Land. There is only one problem—Moses wanted no part of the assignment. After coming up with a myriad of excuses, Moses finally pleaded with God, saying,

> "Oh, my Lord, I am not eloquent, either in the past or since You have spoken to Your servant, but I am slow of speech and of tongue." Then the LORD said to him, "Who has made man's mouth? Who makes him mute, or deaf, or seeing, or blind? Is it not I, the LORD? Now therefore go, and I will be with your mouth and teach you what you shall speak." (Exodus 4:10–12)

Despite God's promised provision, His offer is met with this reply from Moses: "Oh, my Lord, please send someone else" (Exodus 4:13).

Then the Lord gives Moses exactly what he needs—community. A companion, a mouthpiece, in the form of Aaron. Check it out:

> Is there not Aaron, your brother, the Levite? I know that he can speak well. Behold, he is coming out to meet you, and when he sees you, he will be glad in his heart.

> You shall speak to him and put the words in his mouth, and I will be with your mouth and with his mouth and will teach you both what to do. He shall speak for you to the people, and he shall be your mouth, and you shall be as God to him. (Exodus 4:14–16)

They would be in community together, serving the Lord together, and it's exactly what was needed to follow the call of God.

I see this in the ministry where I serve. On Monday mornings when our food pantry receives a shipment of food from the regional food bank, those of us in the church office down the hall know because of the laughter that comes from the group that's putting it all away. The women who lead our women's retreat consistently report how serving on the planning team binds them together and enables them to see God work in ways they never imagined. Our staff shares not only laughs but also fervently prays for one another and walks alongside one another in life and ministry challenges. This is all experienced because serving together, shoulder to shoulder, facilitates these things.

If you are a part of a church family, then you see this alive in your location as well. And having seen it in a number of locations, I'm convinced it's true. People who serve together experience a level of care for one another and a sense of living in and practicing community with one another that those who don't serve simply do not experience.

Now, I'm fully aware that serving together isn't easy. In fact, it's the opposite. Between busy schedules and finding a place that fits individual tastes and gifts, service can be a real challenge. My personal struggle is that for the sake of efficiency, I think it's just easier to do things on my own. What a mistake! Not only does that rob other people of rewarding opportunities to serve, but it also robs me of the power of serving with other people. And truth be told—the results are often better when others make it happen.

Perhaps you're a church leader who struggles with the challenge of getting people to serve. Trust me, I know the struggle. A game-changing shift our congregation made recently is to invite new and potential volunteers into limited time or minimal responsibility roles, that is, to help with one event or to serve for a short length of time. We found that people are more willing to say yes to bite-size opportunities. People who agreed to help in our pantry once then found it easier to commit to once a month. People who agreed to be a Sunday School teaching assistant then found it rewarding to step into leading a class once they got a handle on it.

What's true for those ministry leaders is also true for you. If you're looking to experience the richness of serving, and the benefits of serving with others, but don't know where to start, I encourage you—just start somewhere. For example, volunteering to serve at the local homeless shelter every week is a huge step, one so big it could paralyze you.

Playing Bible Baseball or Basketball

But serving once a month or even once a quarter is manage-able—and most of all, it's worth it. You'll be a step closer to experiencing the power of being in community, and your contribution will be significant and influential.

Hear the heart of the apostle Paul and his love for the Church in Philippi, a church he had labored with and with whom he had built rich community. His words in Philippians 1 reflect the personal impact their time together had on him:

> I thank my God in all my remembrance of you, always in every prayer of mine for you all making my prayer with joy, because of your partnership in the gospel from the first day until now. And I am sure of this, that He who began a good work in you will bring it to completion at the day of Jesus Christ. It is right for me to feel this way about you all, because I hold you in my heart, for you are all partakers with me of grace, both in my imprisonment and in the defense and confirmation of the gospel. For God is my witness, how I yearn for you all with the affection of Christ Jesus. (Philippians 1:3–8)

From Bible times through today, community is practiced and realized best among people who serve together.

This won't always be simple and easy. The evil one thrives on division and self-centeredness and will do anything he can to thwart community. When you dance with some-one, you are likely to step on the other's toes. Challenge and conflict will happen. However, as a friend and partner in the ministry Les Stroh likes to say, "Conflict is inevitable; enemies are optional." Well said.

It's important to remember that the Church is comprised entirely of sinful people, and sinful people don't cease being sinful when they join a faith family or when they step into a leadership role. We know this, but church hurts sting, doubly so, it seems, because we feel like Christians should know and act differently and better. Yet thanks be to God, Jesus forgives us, brings us into community with Him, and keeps us in His Church by His grace.

Jesus is doing this with you. I pray you find your identity in Him. Regardless of your past or your present, He makes a place for *you*. I pray that you develop an understanding of belonging in Him that is unparalleled. In Him you are invited to know both who you are and whose you are. Finally, I pray that you are led to discover anew the joy it is to be within His Body, His family, His community, His Church. Because our Lord ordains it, practicing and living in community unlocks abundant joy.

Ancient Greek philosopher Plato (428–348 BC) is thought to have defined the longing of humanity in this way, "Man is a being in search of meaning." Later on, Early Church Father Augustine (AD 354–430) brought light to this search, powerfully reflected on finding hope in Christ Jesus, writing, "Thou hast made us for Thyself, O Lord, and our heart is restless until it finds its rest in Thee."

Listen, and follow, as the Lord invites you to find what you are searching for in Him.

> You will seek Me and find Me, when you seek Me with all your heart. (Jeremiah 29:13)

> All that the Father gives Me will come to Me, and whoever comes to Me I will never cast out. (John 6:37)

> Ask, and it will be given to you; seek, and you will find; knock, and it will be opened to you. For everyone who asks receives, and the one who seeks finds, and to the one who knocks it will be opened. (Matthew 7:7–8)

Questions to invite reflection and conversation

1. In what ways is worship restful for you? Which parts of your worship experience recharge you?

2. What sometimes gets in the way of your finding rest and Sabbath in worship?

3. Which Christian relationships are especially meaningful for you? How have you experienced "iron sharpens iron"?

4. Do you feel you need to pursue more or increased depth in your Christian relationships? If so, what steps might you take to get there?

5. When have you experienced that serving alongside others brings a deeper sense of community for you?

6. What is one step you could see yourself taking to increase your sense of community with the Lord and with others?

LEADER GUIDE

Chapter 1

1. In what ways do you sense loneliness and anxiety on the rise culturally?

Take note of the use of "culturally" in the question. We're not necessarily looking for people to speak about *their* loneliness or anxiety, but rather how they see it *around* them. This makes it easier for people to speak to the issue. Examples include statistics that speak to loneliness and anxiety, suicide rates on the rise, people retreating to distractions on phones, and self-medicating through alcohol or drugs.

2. Where do you see an increase of divisions and a spirit of divisiveness in our world today?

Again, we're looking for examples from culture. This is seen most prominently in the political landscape, yet it's not just politics. People seem forced to take sides on issues of many kinds, and you are either in one camp or the other. Meanwhile, the language about "the others" is increasingly vitriolic. This includes politics, but also stances on social issues, raising children, even which chicken sandwich or hummus you prefer!

3. **What impact is tribalism having on our culture? How is it leading us to think negatively about others?**

This spirit of tribalism and divisiveness is leading us to think of others as the enemy. Instead of celebrating what we have in common, we are pitted against one another. This is not how the Lord invites us to be and live. The New Testament is full of wonderful examples of looking past cultural/societal divisions and celebrating what we share as God's children. See Galatians 3:28–29.

4. **Why do you think unity was so important to Jesus? Why did He pray to God the Father for it?**

Unity was important to Jesus because at its core, the work of Jesus on the cross and through the empty tomb is a unifying work! His work unites us and brings us into His family, where we celebrate and work to preserve our unity in Him. The work of the evil one is a work that sows discord and division. Unity is a gift of God to be received and celebrated, and Jesus prays that this might continually be our reality as His people.

5. **This chapter listed concepts of community that are found throughout the Bible. Which example was new or most striking to you?**

Here we are looking for people to choose from the list of biblical examples of community and share which was most impactful for them. The list was comprised of the following:

- The Creation Story
- The Twelve Tribes of Israel
- Jesus Calling Disciples
- Jesus Sending Disciples
- Jesus in Gethsemane
- Community in the Early Church
- Looking Ahead to Heaven

Chapter 2

1. **In which way have you experienced "the world beating up on you"—through comparison, the quest for achievement, or feelings of inadequacy?**

Look for answers that speak to the pain and hurt people experience from the brokenness of the world. These include comparing ourselves to others and feeling as though we fall short, our constant pursuit of excellence or perfection, and feelings of guilt, shame, or "less than" that weigh on us.

2. **How is the forgiveness Christ Jesus won for you especially meaningful for you? How does it change you?**

Forgiveness gives us a new sense of identity and belonging. It means that we are no longer defined by what we've done or failed to do, but rather we are recipients of the grace and love of the God of all creation. This becomes who we are and how we think of ourselves. It changes us because we no longer view ourselves using the world's metrics. Instead, we rest in who God declares us to be.

3. **What does it mean to you to find your sense of identity and belonging in Jesus Christ?**

Identity is how we think of and define ourselves; belonging is where we fit in. The world has answers for both of these, but Jesus Christ has the best answers. When we find our identity in Him, we anchor ourselves in something that cannot change (1 Peter 1:3–4), and we are brought into His family. We belong there, solely because God's work has made it so.

4. **We defined sanctification as "the steady process God works in us to align us more and more with Him and His will for us." How do you sense His sanctifying work in your life? How is He shaping you and drawing you closer to Him and His will?**

God's sanctifying work happens through regularly being in His Word, receiving the Lord's Supper, and remembering our Baptism. Through these Means of Grace, He strengthens our faith and draws us closer to Him. These Means of Grace are supplemented by our own response: confident prayer and living in community. This means we think differently, we speak differently, we act differently. We are more hopeful, we have an increased faith and trust in God, and we are more at peace.

5. **How does the lengthy history of God working through imperfect people bring you comfort?**

We ought not think God works only through people who "have it all together." Rather, God uses us despite our imperfections. See 2 Corinthians 4:6–9. He has made us part of the Body of Christ, through faith in Jesus, and now as part of the Body we serve Him and serve others. This should bring us comfort, because serving in God's kingdom is dependent on His work, not on ours.

Chapter 3

1. **Have you had an experience where you felt like an outsider? How did it feel?**

Feeling like an outsider is an experience common to many. It can include starting in a new school or a new job, joining a different team, or moving to a new neighborhood. This often makes us feel inadequate, uncomfortable, and unsure of ourselves.

2. **Which element of the Bible's use of body imagery to describe the Church is most meaningful for you?**

Elements include how one's past status, or even one's present status, does not disqualify him or her from being part of the Body, how each part is equally celebrated and important, and how each part is designed to be in concert with one another and is truly indispensable.

3. **Have you ever had a powerful group experience? Why do you think it was so impactful?**

Survey the group to have them provide examples of memorable group experiences. These might include being part of a family, a congregation, a sports team, a theater troupe, a team at work, or the like. These are often impactful because you feel like you are making a difference, strong bonds are created, and you feel a sense of accomplishment.

4. Do you ever find yourself growing weary? Who are the people who "hold up your hands"?

The multitude of demands placed on us can have us running on empty and feeling weary. This can be due to stress and obligations at home, work, or school. We face health challenges, financial setbacks, and uncertainty regarding the future. In the midst of all this, the Lord has placed people around us to "hold up our hands," including spouse, children, parents, extended family members, friends, co-workers, neighbors, and the like.

5. Where and with whom might you find yourself sitting, listening, and asking questions as Jesus does in Luke 2?

In a culture where everyone seems to have an opinion and then freely shares it, "sitting, listening, and asking questions" is a lost art. Encourage the group to practice listening and to receive the blessings of doing so. Examples might include with family members, especially older ones, co-workers, neighbors, and anyone with an interesting story to share.

Chapter 4

1. **In what ways is worship restful for you? Which parts of your worship experience recharge you?**

Worship is a place where little is expected of us; it's a place where we come and receive. God does the work, and we benefit from it. It's a place to pause, not be busy, and escape the demands of life. Elements of the worship experience include singing, listening to the reading of God's Word and the sermon, receiving the Lord's Supper, praying, confessing, and receiving absolution.

2. **What sometimes gets in the way of your finding rest and Sabbath in worship?**

Sometimes, it's hard to shut down our minds and come into God's presence to find rest. We might be thinking of problems in our lives, what is upcoming in the week ahead, or even some elements of the Sunday experience that distract us.

3. **Which Christian relationships are especially meaningful for you? How have you experienced "iron sharpens iron"?**

God has given us the gift of Christian friendships. These might be members of your church, Christians friends, neighbors, co-workers, or fellow members of a small group or a

Bible study. Here we experience unity, fellowship, encourage-ment, and even helpful challenging of one another.

4. **Do you feel you need to pursue more or increased depth in your Christian relationships? If so, what steps might you take to get there?**

Authentic and deep Christian community is difficult to find and cultivate, especially in a world of division and divi-siveness. This question is designed to help people take an inventory of whether they have a strong sense of Christian community or if they feel it is lacking. If they desire a richer sense of Christian community, encourage praying, sharing the need with other Christians and their pastor, and consid-ering who in their life has a walk with Jesus Christ that they admire—that might be a good person to reach out to.

5. **When have you experienced that serving alongside others brings a deeper sense of community for you?**

Serving binds people together. Examples include teach-ing Sunday School, playing an instrument or singing in a choir, serving in a food pantry or homeless shelter, traveling on a church mission trip, or being on a staff or leadership team.

6. **What is one step you could see yourself taking to increase your sense of community with the Lord and with others?**

One goal of this book is that it leads to action. Sometimes, action—or any kind of change—can be intimidating. This question encourages each participant to consider an action step that leads to a richer sense of community with the Lord and with others. Steps with the Lord might include regular worship, joining a Bible study or small group, or serving in a new way. Steps with others might include reaching out for coffee and conversation, reconnecting with an old friend, or committing to more regularly "sitting, listening, and asking questions."